iTwit

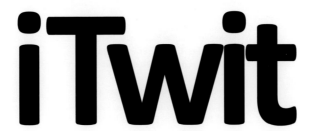

iTwit

Fake Apps for Genuine Idiots

Fintan Coyle & Dan Louw

JOHN BLAKE

Published by John Blake Publishing Ltd,
3 Bramber Court, 2 Bramber Road,
London W14 9PB, England

www.johnblakepublishing.co.uk

First published in paperback in 2010

ISBN: 978 1 84358 282 3

British Library Cataloguing-in-Publication Data:

A catalogue record for this book is available from the British Library.

Design by Phudge Design

Typesetting by www.envydesign.co.uk

Printed in Great Britain by Thomson Litho Ltd. East Kilbride, Scotland

1 3 5 7 9 10 8 6 4 2

All photographs reproduced courtesy of the authors with the
exception of the photograph on page 91 reproduced courtesy
of IgnitePhotography.co.uk

Papers used by John Blake Publishing are natural, recyclable products
made from wood grown in sustainable forests. The manufacturing processes
conform to the environmental regulations of the country of origin.

Fintan Coyle

As a medical student, Fintan Coyle wrote, directed and performed in Edinburgh Fringe comedies. As a doctor, he was twice nominated for The PPA Columnist Of The Year for his journalism. On TV, he co-presented the teenage advice show *Speakeasy!* with Emma Forbes. Since leaving medicine, he has written comedy and created formats for broadcast and digital media. He co-wrote the BBC Radio Four operatic sitcom *Taking It Up The Octave* and co-devised the quiz format *The Weakest Link* for BBC TV. His cult medical sitcom *tlc* was broadcast on BBC2.

Dan Louw

By day, Dan Louw comes up with TV ideas for a production company in North London. By night, he sleeps. As a producer, director and development wonk he's made programmes for all of the major UK broadcasters, covering subjects as diverse as chronic flatulence, extra nipples, Japanese fish and transvestite nannies in the American Deep South. He's a sometime stand-up comedian and he really wishes you would buy this book, and thanks you if you already have.

Acknowledgements

A big thank you to everyone who helped us put the book together, especially: Katharine, John, Tina, Stu, Lissa, Dauda, Emily L, Emily LG, Luke, Charlie, Carrie, Nick S, Nick C, Nick H, Silke, Celine, Dave, Matt, Peter, Natalie, Kevin, Kris, Adrian, James, Chris G, Andrew, Annelise, Ben, Dan R, Ayten, Melody, Andy R, Daisy, Larissa, Helen, Isis, Louise, Caris, Aidan, Fry the cat and Lola the dog.

Respect to our agent KT Forster who brought us together and worked so hard to get us published. Cheers to everyone at John Blake for believing in the idea and not asking too many questions. Finally, our gratitude to our amazing designer Andrew Gordon, whose talent and attitude is unmatched amongst anyone we've worked with.

Fintan personally thanks Louise, for all her love and support throughout the years.

Dan personally thanks everyone at North One for putting up with his nonsense; also to White Cat and Heurelho Gomes. Thanks most of all to Lauren, whose amazingness is too vast to detail here.

Introduction

Thank you for purchasing the analogue version of this book. Unfortunately, due to technological limitations, the crapps previewed here will exhibit limited functionality. No amount of prodding, swiping or licking of the pages will make them work. So, please stop it – you're just making a scene...

iTwit was inspired by both the genius (and idiocy) of the technology that we have come to love (and hate). Most of these ideas are too stupid to exist. Nearly all of them are technologically impossible. But we hope that there's at least a couple that will make you think 'wouldn't it be awesome if that really existed?' We think it would be awesome too, not least because at £1.99 per crapp, we could be making serious money!

Of course, most commercial apps for mobiles are carefully vetted for functionality, decency, and appropriateness. For *iTwit* the only restrictions were that they were written in English and that no animals were harmed in making the screenshots. And none were – except maybe Bella on page 23, who almost died. Sadly, we then had to 'let nature take its course' when the vet gave his estimate for the treatment bill. Does that *really* count as 'harmed'? We think not.

The human race, on the other hand, didn't get off so lightly. Particular commiserations go out to the guy that we electrocuted on page 15; and the family whose house we burgled on page 92.

Be warned, though. Many of the crapps within this book are puerile and idiotic, which is what happens when you allow puerile idiots to write a book. Some crapps display attitudes and behaviours that we, the authors, despise and deplore. Please be assured that we do not – and never will – condone fraud, cannibalism or mucking about on public transport.

We sincerely hope you enjoy this collection, and if all it does is help legitimise your interest in collecting pubic hair, well, then all our labours will have been worth it...

Contents

Toddler 2.0

Throw away the teething rings and teddy bears, because baby's got his first smartphone...

£80.08

We understand how terrible the 'terrible twos' can be – it's a confusing time in your life where you're constantly crying, crapping yourself, or crying because you've crapped yourself. If you're going to make it through infancy with your dignity intact, you need a strategy – a way of reminding your exhausted parents exactly who wears the nappies around here! Download Toddler 2.0 onto the smartphone they bought you after that almighty tantrum, and follow the brightly-coloured, fully-illustrated instructions. Let this unique 'todcast' teach you to think like an adult and sit back and wait for the toys, lollipops and cartoons to come flooding in...

Features
- Supermarket Frenzy suggests the items on the shelves that you may decide to have tantrums over whilst trapped in the trolley seat
- Keeps track of mummy and daddy's fluctuating stress levels and reminds you to go absolutely crazy just when they're hitting their lowest ebb
- Chew Choosers selects items to put in your mouth to freak out your parents – from earthworms to grandma's antique jewellery
- Takes the edge off of your parents' attempt to scold you by playing jaunty nursery rhymes over their voices and replacing their angry faces with images of stuffed toys!
- Fussy Eater tells you the foodstuffs to refuse that will cause maximum distress your parents

User Reviews

***
This crapp encouraged me to express my inner rage by crayoning all over the newly painted nursery walls. That will teach mum to give me a new little brother...

****
Has taught me the value of sharing nicely. I have now shared nits, threadworms and impetigo with the playgroup.

Mummy and daddy are refusing to download it for you? Car keys go bye-bye...

Customers Also Bought
Pimp My Tricycle; 1,000 Things To Ask 'Why?' About; Tooth Fairy – The Evidence

Toddler 2.0

I'm Not Eating That!

CARROT BATONS: Too orange - Request chips
BABY SWEETCORN - Yuk! Stick down underpants
CHEAP VALUE HAM - Demand Chateaubriand steak (medium rare)
SERVING REQUEST: *"Me want ketchup! Now!"*

Sweet Talking

DESIRED ITEM:
Lollipop

TIMESCALE FOR REQUEST:
Now!

REASON FOR REQUEST:
Because I want it!

You Don't Scare Me, Mummy

CHOSEN MASK:
✓ Fred the Ted   Hunny the Bunny

CHOSEN SOUNDTRACK
The Happy Clappy Bing Bong Song

3+ Ratings ★★★

Blame
Imaginary Friend

Fill Nappy

Cat Scan

What does your cat do all day? Well, we think he's cheating on you...

£0.99

Your cat is laughing at you. It might sound like gentle purring, but it's actually a stream of evil chuckling at your abject stupidity. Every night he eats your food, craps on your lawn, shags underneath your window and then goes next door for even more food! What's more, he can't believe he's getting away with it! Now's the time to stop him – get your paws on Cat Scan, the only bit of kit that shows you exactly what he's up to when he's not leeching off you. Wipe that smirk off his furry little face and let him know that he won't always land on his feet!

Features
- Simply tie your phone to his torso while he's asleep and use the GPS and night vision functions to track his every move
- Keeps tracks of his wilder impulses and warns you whenever he tears apart a sparrow and leaves it in your slippers as a 'present'
- Food Whore. You may be feeding him the finest premium cat food 'because of his delicate digestion', but just wait until you see the sort of grub he is woofing down everywhere else!
- Find out what he's actually calling you to your face! Learn 'Catois' – the hyper-aggressive feline slang he hurls at you every time he meows

Upgrade
Old Lady Edition tracks up to 500 cats, even the dead ones behind the sofa...

Kick that no good, cheating kitty to the kerb – and tell him to take that chewed-up catnip mouse with him...

Customer Reviews
***
I was attacked by a lion while on safari. As he licked my skin off I was able to decipher that he thought I tasted like chicken. Cheeky!

**
My attitude to Ginger changed the day that Cat Scan revealed that his affectionate 'Meow' roughly translates as, 'Oi, you bastard!'

Customers Also Bought
Teach Yourself Gerbiling; My Pet Ringworm; Woof Justice

Kit Out Your Cat

Danger: Only 8 Lives Left!

Kitty Cam

TRANSLATING CATOIS:

'Yo, bitch! Where the Catty Chunks at? You best get yo' self outta MY CHAIR and fix ME a snack. Don't make me have to scratch yo' ass.'

Cat-tivity

01:24AM Sneaked into Number 25, and ate 12 grams of Ginger's food

10:35PM Fought with Tiddles. Won.

10:38PM Sprayed on Tiddles' territory

11:31PM Disemboweled frog

63:34AM Fought Tiddles again. Won.

895 Ratings ⭐⭐⭐⭐

Clean Arse with Tongue

Cough Up Furball

Spam Tracker

Because it can't all be a con...can it?

FREE

Every day your inbox is full to bursting with no-strings-attached offers of sex, drugs, pornography and cash from Nigeria. Every day you ignore them. But what if there really was a once-in-a-lifetime opportunity hidden among the deluge of scams? Don't let **your** chance to strike it **rich** slip through your fingers! Provide for your future with the only proven personal spam management system in the whole world that **you** have been **exclusively** chosen to receive at **no cost** whatsoever! Spam Tracker is the **only** virtual accountant that responds to every email as if it's a 100% genuine offer. Spam Tracker – as tasty and versatile as the meat product to which it owes its name!

Features
- Opens communications with distant relatives of former members of West African governments and invests your money in fees that may (or may not) help secure you millions of dollars
- Uses your credit card to purchase dodgy pharmaceuticals that will either cure your erectile dysfunction or cause your kidneys to fail!
- Enters you into bogus competitions to win MP3 players and 3D TVs that never arrive! And remember – more entries equals more offers!
- Takes at face value requests to enter your security details into websites supposedly set up by your bank

Customer Reviews
**
This offer sounded too good to be true – and it was. All I got when I downloaded this crapp was blurry hardcore pornography.

*****
Praise be to you and the highest Lord of Jesus. Friend, I am contacting you with an offer that will be most felicitous for us and you. My father – former Prime Minister of Nqwalaland...

Hey, gullible! Rub your finger on this page for your chance to win a car!

Customers Also Bought
How To Win A Lottery You've Never Entered; Pass On My Passwords; The Crapp That Does Absolutely Nothing

Spam Tracker

Spam Box `Reply`

CashGiveaway@...
Subject: **Free money for free**
Pay nothing! Just send us some money!

WeRYourBank@...
Subject: **SECURITY ALERT!**
We need all your bank passwords just to
check their spellings again....

EZWinLottery@...
Subject: **You won loads of cash!**
So much that it will cost you thousands
to freight it over in a container ship!

WeRecruitPeopleLike@...
Subject: **Become a Qualified GP Locum**
In just a few minutes! Big money for
weekend shifts

Real Lottery (Honestly)@...
Subject: **Free Super Jackpot Lottery Fund**
Your credit card number is your ticket!

Scammy Mc Scam@...
Subject: **This is NOT a 419 Scam**
Send us your money and we'll prove it!

You've Got Mail `Tell Wife`

Souleymane

Subject: **Greetings from Lagos**

My dear friend, I have received your advance of
£12,000.
I regret that I will no longer be participating in
our business transaction as the entire process
has been a scam.
Thank God for your eternal stupidity, S.

Skank Manager

Out

Introduction fee to UglyRussianWives.com......£457

Penis Enlarging...£608

Security fees advanced to relative of
Nigerian oil baron.................................£18,000

In

Winnings from Spanish lottery..............£370,000

Hidden fortune from relative of
Nigerian oil baron............................£2,700,000

6309 Ratings ★★★★★

Buy degree from
University of Pangaea

Find singles in
your area

eSpoon

Forgot your fork?
Keep your hair on!

£0.99

Our mastery of cutlery is the one thing that separates us from the brute beasts upon whose sweet, juicy flesh we dine. eSpoon saves you the humiliation of having to eat with your fingers, by turning your smartphone into the largest ladle you ever saw. Simply use your smartphone to scoop your meal into your mouth – chew, swallow and repeat! Cutlery has never been so glamorous, so expensive and so likely to subject your mouth to a series of painful electric shocks.

Features
- Handles most meals with ease – except soup...
- Displays thousand of different spoons on your phone screen
- Enjoy the clinking sound of stainless steel tapping against your plate with our range of realistic digital sound effects
- Mashes your food into manageable pieces – simply drive your phone into your meal with enough force to squash it
- Rapidly swirl your phone around any hot drink to engage the in-built stirring function

User Reviews
*****
My stomach was distended, flies were buzzing round my head and Irish pop stars were putting on a concert for me. If I hadn't downloaded eSpoon I would have starved to death...

*
I had tried almost everything as surrogate cutlery – lollysticks, scissors, severed hands, you name it. Nothing had worked... and neither did this.

*
I tried to use eSpoon to cook up heroin and ended up incinerating my communal squat.

Totally dishwasher safe ◆

Customers Also Bought
I Can't Believe It's Not a Butter Knife; My First Cheeseboard; iShank

◆ may result in reduced functionality

eSpoon

Suggested Product Use

Goldilocks Mode
Eat!

- Too Hot
- Just Right
- Too Cold

Porridge Temperature

Spoon Selection

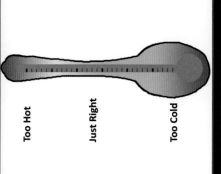

Era: Late Edwardian Dessert Spoons

193 Ratings ★★★

Find Fork Handles

Mack the Knife

Ultimate Cock Fighter

Virtual pet, realistic violence!

£2.99

At last, a faithful simulation of cockfighting – the ancient pastime of poultry-based pugilism! Illegal in many so-called 'civilised' countries, cock-fighting remains a compelling and exciting spectacle all around the world. Now you have the chance to rear your own fighting rooster from egg to ultimate victory. Just link up smartphones, bring your cock to attention and let the feathers fly! You will be delighted to find your cock responding to the most subtle of hand movements as you peck, gauge and lacerate at your opponent's paltry poultry. Just cock-a-doodle-do-it now!

Features
- Raise a variety of exotic fighting cock breeds
- Devise your cock's own intense physical training regimen
- Choose from a selection of designer comb and wattles
- 'Rooster booster' power-ups available
- Unlock additional weaponry including gaffs, cockspurs, long spurs, short spurs and machine guns
- Fight in a variety of exotic venues including Latin America, Southeast Asia, Pakistan, the Philippines and a disused barn in Kent, England
- Full control over tactics including the pecking order and crowing rights

Reviews
****
My cock was small but managed to send five roosters to the cooking pot before I had to wring its neck after it got both eyes pecked out by a White Leghorn built like a brick shit-house. Bring it on!

***
Our plucky bantam bled to death after a gruelling grudge match against a rampant Rock Island Red. As my nine-year-old said, 'I will be avenged you mangy motherf***er!'

****
Would it be possible to introduce to the legs of gamecocks the unique sharp knives (or 'taji') as used in Bali? It's a wonderful variation of the sport.

As secretly enjoyed by vegetarians!

Customers Also Bought:
Pitbull Party; Dolphin Netter; Kitten Karnage

Grow Your Cock   Next

You have hatched!

Feed	Water
Groom	Tickle
Pinch	Boil Siblings
Deny Sunlight	Dose with Rat Hormones

Customise Your Cock

Colour

Weapons

Combs

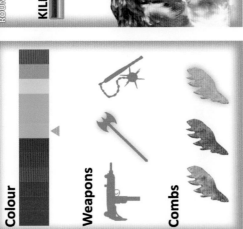

Hardcore Cock-on-Cock Action

ROUND 2

32

KILLACOCK LEVEL 19
SPECIAL

FEATHERS 'THE BASTARD' MCTAVISH LEVEL 24
SPECIAL

182 Ratings ★★★★

Run About with No Head

Order Battery Hens

YouPube

*They're short, they're curly and they're absolutely **everywhere**!*

£5.55

Have you ever picked up a bar of soap and found it speckled with pubic hairs that simply couldn't be yours? Don't waste valuable brainpower trying to figure whose nether regions it came from. Download YouPube and receive a full DNA analysis of the donor within seconds. No matter where you find a pube (be it between your teeth, or on your vicar's dog collar) you'll know instantly who has been doing the minging moulting.

Features
- Individually traces each hair to its originator and assesses structural integrity to reveal whether the specimen was shed routinely or removed by force...
- Maintains a selection of your favourite found hairs in a stunning High Definition gallery you'll want to show the grandkids
- Displays all the fascinating and vital statistics about your fuzzle collection – from the exact hair count, to how many times they would circle the earth if straightened and laid out follicle to tip
- Pube Cataloguer encourages you to collect ever more unusual and exotic pubic hairs, including those of the apes, albinos and hermaphrodites
- Celebrity Pubipedia is a comprehensive compendium of the most famous pubic hairs in the world including The One True Pube held in secret Vatican archives

User Reviews
*****
Pube collecting is a wonderful hobby for all members of the family. All you need is a pair of nail scissors and a keen eye.

*****
I now have nearly 500 different types of pubic hair. I can't wait until I can grow my own.

***
Analysed a pube in my wife's undies and it turned out to be from the milkman. I can't think why she was letting him try them on...

Found one in the binding of this book? It's your flatmate's...

Customers Also Bought
Emission Impossible; Prolapse Pro; Toilet Unblocker Plus

The Pubenheim Gallery

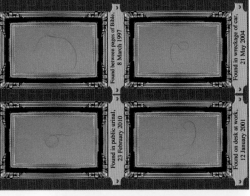

Found between pages of Bible
8 March 1997

Found in wreckage of car,
21 May 2004

Found in public urinal,
23 February 2010

Found on desk at work,
12 January 2001

There's a Pube in My Soup...

Initial Report Complete
746 hairs clipped from the
mons pubis area
Likeliest culprit:
The waiter you moaned at

Whose Hairs?

- Pudendal
- 55 mm long
- coarse diameter with prominent
  diameter variation and buckling
- medulla is broad
- asymmetrical cross section
- spiralling tufted
- folliticular tags present

Analysis Complete
John from Accounts
or
A Western Lowland Gorilla

7843 Ratings ★★★★

Adjust Merkin

Go Brazilian

Cattle Prod

People take you more seriously when you've just zapped them in the face.

£1.99

Do you find it hard to get people's attention? Do you find it frustrating when your family don't listen to you? Do you wish there was a physically debilitating – yet non-lethal – method of asserting your authority? Now there is. Cattle Prod fires a spark of iridescent blue electricity out of the end of your phone, right into the jugular of the latest person to have pissed you off. In just a couple of jolts you'll notice people are choosing their words more carefully and, in some cases, avoiding you altogether!

Features
- Light up your friends with a choice of colours and patterns that will delight bystanders and bring a smile to the lips of arresting officers
- Stand clear! Restart the hearts of collapsed pedestrians with the 'chest paddles' defibrillator function. That which doesn't kill them will make them stronger!
- Take it down a notch or two with our child-friendly function, allowing your offspring to shock their teachers and friends with a low voltage dose
- Out for the count! Make long car journeys a breeze by rendering noisy family members immobile

User Reviews
***
Great fun, but don't make the same mistake I did and forget to lock your phone before you put it in your pocket.

*
I thought Cattle Prod would be the perfect way to keep my factory workers on their toes. Unfortunately productivity is down twenty-five per cent on account of one in four of them being dead now.

*****
That flasher will definitely think twice about exposing himself again...

The crapp the United Nations Human Rights Commission tried to ban!

Customers Also Bought
Waterboarder Pro; Taze Me, Please Me; eBaton

Set Phasers to Fun!

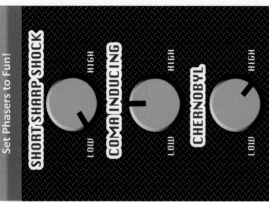

SHORT SHARP SHOCK — LOW / HIGH

COMA INDUCING — LOW / HIGH

CHERNOBYL — LOW / HIGH

Phwoar! What a Stunner!

What's the loss of sight in one eye/infertility between friends?

Shock Tactics

SHOCK LEVEL 150 volts
REASON: DIDN'T LAUGH AT YOUR JOKE

403 Ratings ⭐⭐⭐⭐⭐

ZZZAAAAPPP

PZZZTTT

OCD OMG!

*Get the **must have** crapp of the year, or spend all night worrying about it...*

£1.11

Are you a laid-back, relaxed, chilled-out underachiever without a care in the world? Then maybe you need to be a bit more OCD – the hottest new personality trait in showbiz! Don't be left behind in the evolutionary stakes by an ever-worrying, all-tidying master race. With a hint of Obsessive-Compulsive Disorder, the world sparkles with infinite possibility – everywhere you look there's a sock drawer to sort, a carpet to vacuum and a litter bin to rearrange according to the monetary value of the items contained therein. With this augmented reality crapp you will instantly have a thousand more things to worry about in your life.

Features
- Hold your phone up to any domestic scene and it instantly logs all of the things you'll be fretting about when you leave the house
- Constantly schedules alarms to remind you that you might have left the oven on, not set the burglar alarm, or forgotten to turn your taps off
- Shows up the hidden germs that the naked eye can't see so that you are immediately compelled to smear every surface with anti-bacterial hand lotion
- Immediately identifies DVD collections that you could sort alphabetically and wardrobes that you can reorder according to colour and/or season
- Cycles through the contents of your fridge and goes absolutely batshit-crazy just because the butter is one day past its sell-by date...

User Reviews

Don't forget to read this 8,000 times...

****
I downloaded this and now I'll only have things beginning with 'O' in my house. I have an orange grove in my garden, an octopus in my bath and an orangutan in my bedroom!

****
Thanks to OCD OMG! I'm living in a plastic bubble in my bedroom, refusing to leave the house and slowly starving to death. I've never been happier.

Customers Also Bought
My Narcissism Is Better Than Yours; Missed A Personality?; Imaginary Friend Finder

Stated Obsession: The Letter 'P'

Parapet: possible parrot's perch

Parked Cars

Pub (possible puke, piss and pear cider)

Pavement

AVOID STREET!

Filth Finder

THERE ARE CURRENTLY

32,604

types of organism on the screen of this phone.

including:
- MRSA
- FAECAL SPORES
- EAR WAX

Set Your Alarm Bells Ringing

every 5 mins: Did I turn the grill off??

every 10 mins: Did I leave the window open?

every 1 hour: Have rabid dogs broken in and licked everything in my fridge?

708 Ratings ★★

Repeatedly Press Button

Hoard Similar Crapps

Bus-tard

You're only a teenager once, so you might as well be as big a t**t as possible.

£0.99

There are so many thoughts bouncing around the hormonal teenage mind that it's often easy to lose focus on what's really important (i.e. annoying the shit out of people on public transport). Never again pass up the opportunity to wind up the working stiffs on your bus ride home from school! Whether you're into playing loud music, scratching poorly spelled swearwords into glass or setting fire to other passengers' hair, Bus-tard is a one-way ticket to ASBO Central!

Features
- Messes with the equalizer on even the highest-tech phones so that every tune you play through the speakers sounds tinnier and more irritating than the last
- Accurately calculates the chain reaction caused by a single shove to your mate's back. Find out which unlucky passengers they'll be barrelling into and how many things they'll be knocking over on the way!
- Ding ding! Drive the driver mad by ringing the bell every ten seconds without ever taking your hands out of your pockets
- Voice Breaker Plus helps shift your voice to the most irritating octave – allowing you to squeal and squeak at your friends whilst boasting about imaginary sexual encounters!

The most fun you can have on a bus without getting drunk and taking the wheel...

User Reviews

***
I'm a socially maladjusted 43-year-old man and this brilliant crapp has been invaluable in helping me impress, amuse and even impregnate several local delinquents.

*
It's fine for mucking about on a bus. Not so fine if you're part of the security detail on Air Force One.

**
I drive a local mobility vehicle and my life was a lot easier before the OAPs discovered this.

Customers Also Bought
Let's All Have a Pile Up!; Child Seat Ejector Button; Minicabs – Major Accidents

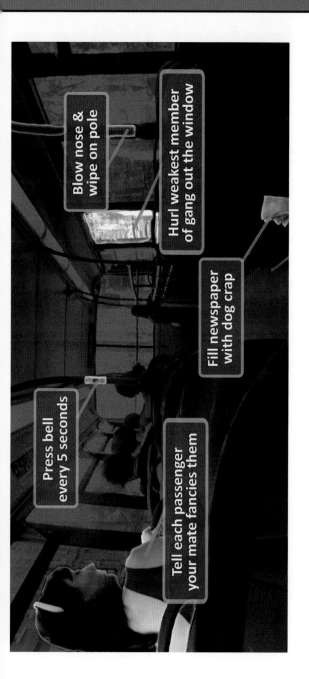

Instant Office Party

Because that arse isn't going to photocopy itself!

£0.99

Do you wish it could be Christmas every day? Do you wish that every boring work day contained the hi-jinks and intoxicated, unprotected sex of the office Christmas party? With Instant Office Party just hike down your trousers, squat over your phone and delight as it becomes the world's smallest photocopier. In seconds you'll have a smudged, black-and-white photo of your backside, ready to email round the entire company!

Features
- Whirrs, clicks and emits a beam of light beneath your squished genitals – just like a real photocopier
- What a load of old arse! – makes enlarged or reduced copies at the touch of a button
- For added hilarity, make use of our enhanced range of sound effects – pass to one of your heavier colleagues and watch their face as the sound of breaking glass fools them into thinking they've busted the phone (and their arse) in one sitting!
- Embarrass colleagues who try it out with the inbuilt cling-on and haemorrhoid detector

User Reviews

***
If you're struggling to bond with a colleague on a trip away with work, this is the ultimate ice breaker.

*
The quality is rubbish – I get much clearer images from the colour copier in my headteacher's office.

***
Great fun – especially when you've just used it and your girlfriend wants to borrow your phone to call her mum!

The most fun you can have with (some of) your clothes on!

Customers Also Bought
1,000 Things To Shout At Women In the Street; Employment Tribunal 101; Go Postal

Party Time!

Capture

Sit on Phone

Email to Boss

Post on Arsebook

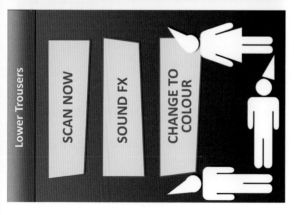

Lower Trousers

SCAN NOW

SOUND FX

CHANGE TO COLOUR

16 Ratings ★★★★

Attend Disciplinary Hearing

Collect P45

Pesticidal Maniac

Turns your home into a scene of unimaginable slaughter.

£2.99

Got ants in your pants? Bugs in your rugs? Rats in your spats? Foxes in your boxes? Mouses in your houses? Don't these lower forms of life understand that we humans are bigger than them, stronger than them and could take them in a fight if it came down to it? Transform your smartphone into a comprehensive pest control professional and show zero tolerance to any species that dares to share your domestic living environment. Reassert the natural order of things and download the crapp that'll kick nature's ass!

Features

- Attracts flies by displaying a wide variety of images no self-respecting bluebottle will be able to resist – from dog turds to rotten meat and fizzy drinks – and then causes them to stick to your screen for you to squish at your convenience
- Customisable blue UV output screen attracts all other insect types and zaps them – just like those lamps posh restaurants have!
- Mousetrap engaged! Stand phone upright and, when a mouse approaches, it will fall over and give it a nasty bump on the head
- Pied Piper function – plays lilting pipe music to attract local rats and makes them follow it to your neighbour's garden pond to be drowned
- Emits ultrasonic repellent noise for larger garden pests such as foxes, badgers and pandas

So effective at exterminating pests that it'll kill you, if it feels it has to…

User Reviews

*****
We were delighted when we discovered it had taken down a grizzly bear. The zookeeper was less impressed…

*
Not child friendly. My two year old nearly lost her foot when it was in mantrap mode.

***
Was no help at all in getting a big arachnid out of my bath. It just shouted 'Spider! Spider!' and fell down the stairs.

Customers Also Bought
Ant Stamper Deluxe; Fox Me Stupid; With Snail & I

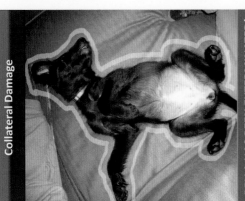

Collateral Damage

BELLA HAS BEEN EXTERMINATED! (mistaken for Giant Horsefly)

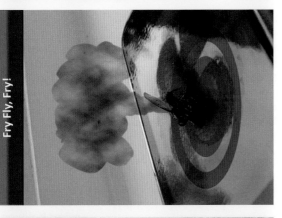

Fry Fly, Fry!

Select Bait

Poultry Poo

All You Can Eat Garbage

Wing of Dead Pigeon

Sheep Shit

Terrier Turd

Dog Diarrhoea

592 Ratings ★★★

Kill One

Kill All

U.O.Me

You can't put a price on friendship – until now!

£0.99

Just had a massive barney with your so called BFF? Sick of the fact that they don't appreciate all of the things you do for them? It was bound to happen – after all, they're nasty and stingy and ugly, and you're great and generous and not ugly. U.O.Me helps you calculate how much your friendship was REALLY worth. Download U.O.Me – because every friENDship has an END.

Features
- Calculates the monetary value of every favour you've ever done for your ex-mate and sends a text message demanding payment
- Simply input your hourly wages and the amount of time spent on each task and this crapp does all the sums for you
- Reclaim every penny of lost earnings that you spent braiding the hair and doing the homework of that stuck up little cow
- Break their legs – at arm's length! Each message alerts local bailiffs, who'll put the squeeze on your friend in the hope of a quick, easy payment

Upgrades
The latest version boosts your claims to incorporate chargeable assets and emotional distress. Lent her your hair strengtheners? Charge up to half of their monetary value every tax year! Cried when she told you her latest sob story? Sue her!

Experience the thrill of cyber bullying at the touch of a button!

User Reviews
***
£714 owed! Take that, Sarah! After all those years of breast-feeding your bloody husband because of his dairy intolerance…

*****
My friend Sharon told me never to tell anyone about what we done to her rich aunt. I've told U.O.Me and now I'll be telling the police unless she gives me £8,000.

Customers Also Bought
How Selfish Can You Be?; Who Needs Friends?; Payback Time

U.O.Me

Turn your BFF into your worst NME

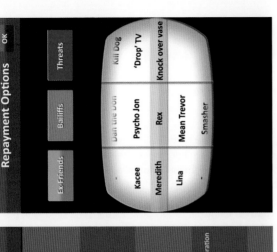

Shaz   Vicki   Bethan

Didn't text back
Too Fat
► Too Skinny
Total bee-yotch
Borrowed my straighteners

Favour Breakdown

Cheryl-Louise
Services Rendered 2009

Drove her to the airport: 3hrs, roundtrip
Potential lost earnings: £26.40
Job at the time: Store Manager, Claire's Accessories

Offered relationship advice: 43mins
Potential lost earnings: £4.56
Job at the time: Tesco, checkout girl

Bridesmaid at her wedding: Several weeks of preparation
Potential lost earnings: £11,800
Job at the time: Sleeping with Kuwaiti men

Repayment Options   OK

Ex-Friends   Bailiffs   Threats

Kacee	Dan the Don	Kill Dog
Meredith	Psycho Jon	'Drop' TV
Lina	Rex	Knock over vase
	Mean Trevor	Smasher

924 Ratings ★★★

Talk to the hand...

'cause the face ain't listening

eGarden

Cover your phone in manure and give it back to the earth!

£0.99

In this age of data limits, video messaging, and social networking it's so hard to find respite from the modern world. We've become so reliant on technology that sometimes you just want to strip naked, run into a forest and cover yourself in moss. But wait! Put your clothes back on and clean yourself off, for with eGarden (the only crapp that's 100% organic and free from harmful pesticides) you can finally get in touch with nature at the touch of a button. Simply download a 'data seed' and plant your phone into a pot with four inches of soil. Then just watch it germinate and grow – you'll be hugging trees and scoffing muesli in no time!

Features
- Choose from tens of different plants to grow on your screen – from crested cockscomb (*Celosia cristata*) to nipplewort (*Lapsana communis*)
- Buy virtual fruit and veg from our dedicated digital greengrocer, then watch it rot into e-compost that will nourish your plants
- Unique dual-hydration technology – either press the dedicated on-screen 'water plant' button, or soak your phone with real liquids, from water to old cups of tea
- Download seed-specific malware protection software to stop your plants from being scoffed by simulated slugs and artificial aphids
- Keen to raise an entire crop of plants? Simply buy a whole batch of phones, download this crapp a thousand times and rent a warehouse!

At last – plants that don't steal our precious water, sunlight or carbon dioxide!

User Reviews

*****
This crapp was quite a little money-spinner. I raised one bushel of digital wheat and managed to trick the European Union into paying me a million pound farm subsidy!

**
Plant recognition is not good. I thought I was growing asparagus. Had I known I was cultivating the carnivorous plant *Canninus scoffum*, then maybe my pet dog would still be with us.

Customers Also Bought
Gangrene Fingers; Tree's Company; Whoreticulture

Money DOES Grow on Trees!

Hydroponic!

You have 235 cannabis plants
You have reached the level of
YARDIE BADMAN

Photo Synthesize

I have sprouted!

- Keep me in a dark room
- Water me occasionally
- Play me krunk & techno

Just Add Water

Tomato Seed	Sunflower Seed
Peyote Cactus	Audrey from 'Little Shop of Horrors'
Seed of Chucky	Seeds of Love

42 Ratings ★★★

Find Dead Mole in Watering Can

Step in a Cat Turd

Hypochondriapp

Because you're sick and you know it.

£9.99

Have you spent the past four years trying to convince specialists that you only have two weeks to live? Are you certain that you have the only rare fatal disease that will not reveal itself in any known medical test? Does your local GP have a restraining order on you? Take control of your soon-to-be-tragically-cut-short life with Hypochondriapp – the ultimate ill-health and disease crapp.

Features
- Accesses World Health Organisation databases to track rare viruses across the world – after all it won't be long before they arrive on your doorstep
- Convinces you that everything you smell, taste, eat and touch causes cancer
- Bar code reader function allows you to analyse all your food purchases for toxic additives, carcinogens, chemicals, enzymes, E numbers, hormones and spermatozoa
- Suggests new and varied food intolerances you may want to develop and bore people with at dinner parties
- Symptom-sorter assumes every minor symptom signifies a major disease and decides whether to call for a routine or priority ambulance visit

Reviews
*****
Thanks to Hypochondriapp I only now realise quite how many potential serious illnesses I might have. It's deeply humbling to think how much the taxpayer will be spending on my unnecessary investigations in the next ten years...

The crapp that probably gives you cystitis...

***
Based on my symptoms diary, it told me that I had Pneumonoultramicroscopicsilicovolcanoconiosis, which was worrying because the harder it is to spell a disease, the more serious it is. Turned out to be hay fever.

Customers Also Bought
Portable Clap Clinic; Complete Home Gynaecologist; Rectal Thermometer Lite

Hypochondriapp

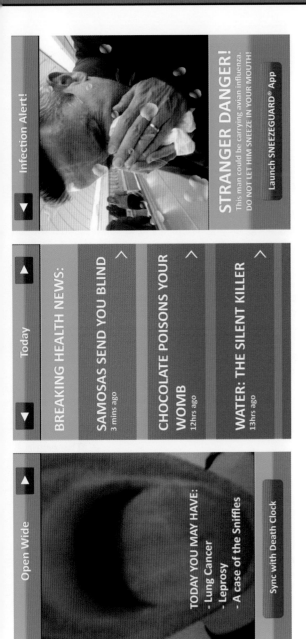

Open Wide ▲

TODAY YOU MAY HAVE:
- Lung Cancer
- Leprosy
- A case of the Sniffles

Sync with Death Clock

▼ **Today** ▲ ▲

BREAKING HEALTH NEWS:

SAMOSAS SEND YOU BLIND
3 mins ago ∧

CHOCOLATE POISONS YOUR WOMB
12hrs ago ∧

WATER: THE SILENT KILLER
13hrs ago ∧

▼ **Infection Alert!**

STRANGER DANGER!
This man could be carrying avian influenza.
DO NOT LET HIM SNEEZE IN YOUR MOUTH!

Launch SNEEZEGUARD® App

83 Ratings ★★

Ram Raid Pharmacy

Book Hospice Bed

Booze Views

The morning after – today!

£1.99

Chaps, have you ever chanced upon the phenomenon of a fugly female becoming increasingly attractive in direct proportion to the amount of alcohol imbibed? Among the drinking classes this is known as the 'beer goggle' effect. Booze Views uses sophisticated algorithms and image manipulation techniques to accurately recreate the devastating loss of discernment that excessive libation can bring. Simply take a discreet photograph of any dodgy-looking bird, and you will be presented with an image of how she will look after four, six or even ten pints of foaming ale. Will the beast turn into a beauty? Only Booze Views has the answer…

Features
- What's yer poison? Input your expected alcohol intake and get a sneak preview of what the lovely lady will look like when you finish that pint of gin…
- Beggars can't be choosers! 'Blue Balls' function factors in your desperation level based on the length of time since you last had sex!
- Spares your blushes with an early warning system that alerts you when you're too drunk for love… Simply breathe on the screen and it'll tell you whether you're risking brewer's droop, or even one of those burps with a bit of sick in them
- Helps you plan a comprehensive escape strategy the next morning, allowing you to slip silently out the back door and locate the nearest taxi service, aspirin dispenser and clap clinic

Reviews

***
Oops! Booze Views claimed that the fat bridesmaid at my best mate's wedding would look like J-Lo after 14 pints. I got so drunk I ended up getting the bride pregnant.

****
I used Booze Views on my own face and realised that it would only take the average women nine Bacardi Breezers to find me attractive. Now I know exactly how many drinks it takes to seal the deal, I never spend a penny more than I have to!

The crapp that's keeping Doncaster pregnant!

Customers Also Bought
Liver Little, Liver Lot; Street Toilet Pro; One More For The Road Traffic Accident

Fugliness Analysis

26%.....Rancid fish wife
34%.....Pre-Op Transexual
40%.....Crocadillapig █

Input Beverages

ENTER ALCOHOL INTAKE

- ▊ Lager
- ♈ Wine
- ▊ Whisky
- ▼ Vodka
- ⚲ Alcopops
- ▊▊ Meths

Projected Attractiveness

after 10 units
possible effects:
sick in mouth

after 20 units
possible effects:
thumb it in soit

after 30 units
possible effects:
mmm... kebab!

18+ Ratings ★★★★

Tell Your Besht Friend

Pfft....hehehe...
muzzlewuzzle!

Dumbphone

Because some phones are too clever for their own good...

£0.99

It's humiliating knowing that something no bigger than your hand is actually cleverer than you are. It hurts that people never ask *you* what time their train is going to get in, or how much *you* think their share of the bill is going to be. No, they only trust information if it comes from your *phone*. Truth is, your mobile is making you look like a complete arsehole. Download this crapp and take that bloody know-it-all smartphone down a peg or two.

Features
- Unpredictive text misspells everything you ever write and transforms even the most lucid text into barely literate gibberish
- Ruins even the simplest of photographs with elementary mistakes – inserts its own 'finger' over the lens and superimposes witless speech bubbles on every snap
- Infantilises your sat nav so that it insists on playing hide and seek with you whenever you're trying to find an important location
- Avidly scans the internet for increasingly idiotic spam to forward to your friends. Overloads your company's email server with hilarious videos of dogs barking along to Britney Spears songs, and other such junk!
- Downloads tunes you absolutely hate, sings them in a high-pitched voice and constantly gets the words wrong

The stupidest thing you can do to your phone without requiring surgery!

User Reviews

*****
My nephew downloaded this and now I can't turn it off because my phone is too stupid to understand the power button. Megalolz!

*****
I have long received censure for my substandard grammar and frequently philistine text utterances, but it would appear that I am so utterly devoid of sense that this crapp serves to render me sagely literate. I am compelled to shake with mirth while rotating on the parquet.

Customers Also Bought
Own Name Reminder; Are U Smarter Than A 12 Week Old?; Learn To Tie Your Own Laces Today!

Photo Fudger
Fix

Dumbphone says: PMSL! I h8 it wen my fingaz get 2 big!?!?

Text Stupidifier

Your text:
Dearest Cassandra – the Philharmonic are doing Mahler at the Royal Albert in the second week of May. I think I'd like to go. *Hast du lust?*

Translation:
Cas - do u wnt 2 c justin beeber? he iz da gr8test! OMG! PMSL! dere iz a dog ova dere doin a pooh!

Warning: Memory Low

1 Missed Call

From That Bloke Who Used To Go Out With Sharon, What Was His Name? You Remember! John Something? No, Ian. Bloody Hell. He's Mates With the One With the Funny Hair and the Brown Teeth...

67 Ratings ★★★

ROFL

LOL

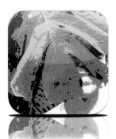

ICanCU

For adults who aren't playing around anymore...

£0.99

There's nothing like a game of hide-and-seek to reinforce the bond between father and son. Trouble is, you let them win a couple of times and they think they're better than you. Trust us – if you show kids even the slightest sign of weakness then the little bastards will walk all over you. ICanCU lets you even the score by bringing cutting-edge military technology into play – uplinking to unmanned spy drones in the sky to hunt your child down like an infidel dog. 'Shoot to kill' air strikes are optional.

Features
- Thermal imaging scans for the body heat of excited boys
- Ultrasensitive audio analyser pinpoints exact sources of childish giggles
- Surveys the house for all potential hiding places and ranks them in likelihood of being reachable within the countdown period
- Works with all known variations of hide and seek, including sardines!
- Can be re-engineered to look for tradesmen hiding in wardrobes, or under the wife's bed

Upgrades
Lost Pet feature seeks out missing small animals – no more finding little Hammy mummified behind the radiator two years after his disappearance.

They can run – but they can't hide!

User Reviews
*
No matter where mummy and I hide, Daddy always finds us ... despite the court order.

***
Thanks to this I was winning every game hands down ... until my eight-year-old was recruited by Mossad and ended up garrotting me during a game of Grandmother's Footsteps.

Customers Also Bought
You're No Son of Mine; Mother's Little Helper; Lose Like a Loser

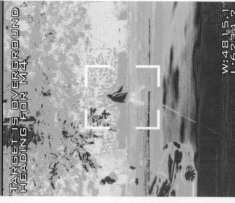

Raw Intel from Unmanned Drone

TARGET IS OVERGROUND
HEADING FOR M4

W:48.15.1
L:6234.2
_TARGET MIB

No Place Left to Hide

BEHIND CURTIANS
Too Fat

INSIDE WARDROBE
Bingo!

UNDER BED
Too Tall

Target Detected

THOMAS
IN THE FRIDGE (AGAIN)

400 Ratings ★★★

Release the Hounds

Report Missing Child

Bunny Boiler

Nothing saves a marriage like a non-existent psycho mistress...

£0.69

Worried that your wife is taking you for granted? Is your love life as uneventful as the West Midlands? What your relationship needs is a spark of jealousy to reignite those lost passions and have you rutting like you were drunk and French. Bunny Boiler makes it seem like you are having it away with a mistress who is quite literally crazy about you! Impress your friends and outrage your wife with the crapp that loves you so much it doesn't think it can take it much longer...

Features
- Customise the personality of your own erratic e-mistress
- Sends you suggestive texts at all hours of the day and night
- Sings your praises as a man and as a mighty lover
- Rings your home number and mysteriously hangs up when your wife answers
- Manipulates photos on social networking sites so it looks like she is constantly at your side
- Bombards you with anguished demands to leave your wife and kids
- Books hotel rooms in the name of 'Mr and Mrs Smith' and charges them to your joint bank account

User Reviews
*
My wife was so convinced that I was having an affair that she went out and shagged my elderly father to get back at me. Grrr!

*****
I love my Bunny Boiler – so much so that I've left my family for her and moved into a flat above a kebab shop...

***
I lent my phone to a friend – big mistake! Now my e-mistress has run off with him and is demanding half of all my assets.

Free restraining order with every download!

Customers Also Bought
Billy No Mates; Everybody's Stalking; No Means 'No'... Or 'Yes'

Bunny Boiler

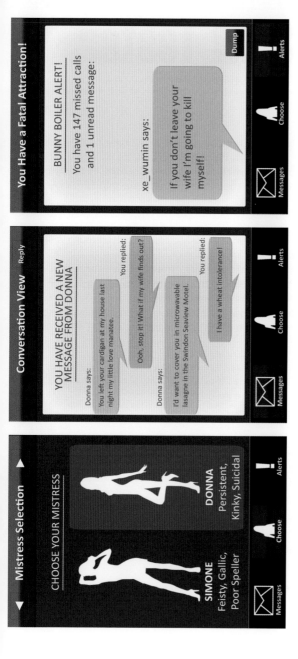

Mistress Selection ▲ ▼

CHOOSE YOUR MISTRESS

SIMONE
Feisty, Gallic,
Poor Speller

DONNA
Persistent,
Kinky, Suicidal

Messages | Choose | Alerts

Conversation View   Reply

YOU HAVE RECEIVED A NEW
MESSAGE FROM DONNA

Donna says:
You left your cardigan at my house last
night my little love manatee.

You replied:
Ooh, stop it! What if my wife finds out?

Donna says:
I'd want to cover you in microwavable
lasagne in the Swindon Seaview Motel.

You replied:
I have a wheat intolerance!

Messages | Choose | Alerts

You Have a Fatal Attraction!

Dump

BUNNY BOILER ALERT!
You have 147 missed calls
and 1 unread message:

xe_wumin says:

If you don't leave your
wife I'm going to kill
myself!

Messages | Choose | Alerts

83 Ratings ★★★★★

Stay late at the
office...again

Appear Distant
and Evasive

Sniff Tester

...because washing's for girls.

£4.02

Late for an important date? Too busy to even look at the washing machine? Use 'Sniff Tester' and stride out of the house with the confidence of knowing that yesterday's undies are still good to go. Your olfactory organ is a treasure trove, full of intrigue and nourishment – don't burden it with menial tasks. Download Sniff Tester – you nose you want to!

Features
- Make manic mornings a breeze, with the only crapp that sifts through your dirty laundry and finds the pants that are right for you
- Run your phone over suspect socks or whiffy Y-fronts and Sniff Tester will instantly tell you whether it's fresh as a daisy, or musky as a hobo's undercarriage
- Never again wash anything unless you really, really have to
- Inbuilt 'Whiffometer' tells you how many more days you can get away with rocking the same chuddies before you get sniffed out

Upgrades
Version 2.3 tells you exactly what your unclean kecks smell like to people up to one hundred metres downwind. V2.4 features a blacklight, like the torch on CSI, that makes your pants look like a Jackson Pollock painting!

User Reviews

*****
Amazing app. Now I never wait for my socks to go hard before I put them in the laundry basket.

*
Tried it on my girlfriend's knickers. Turns out she smells like 'half the premiership'. Confused...

****
Ran it over my mum – said she smelled of rancid beef! ROFL!

Customers Also Bought
Let's Talk About Dingle Berries; Italian Shower; Burpy Turkey

Reveals the scores on your drawers!

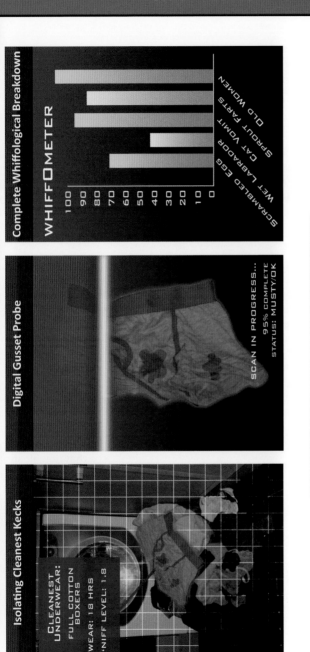

Twat-Nav

Tells you exactly where to go!

£0.99

It's the super-judgemental sat-nav that knows just where you need to go – before you do! Input the co-ordinates to your chosen destination and then watch in horror as Twat-Nav tells you 'not with that haircut you don't!' Do you lack direction? Download Twat-Nav and let the most self-righteous crapp in the business put its foot down – right where it hurts!

Features
- Assesses your weak spots and decides where you need to go to address them
- Analyses your entire phone usage – from your internet searches to your text messages – and forms value judgements about your shortcomings as a human
- Uses this info to suggest 'alternative routes' every time you get into the car. It'll divert you from an important job interview to go and get your stutter sorted. It'll force you to skip your grandmother's funeral to go to a sleazy singles bar. And when it tires of your pathetic floundering, it'll trick you into taking the last ride you'll ever take. 'At the edge of the cliff, keep going…'
- Scared of making tough decisions and confronting difficult issues? Twat-Nav puts itself in the driving seat by hacking all of your other crapps and deleting contact details for all the 'negative' people in your life

Reviews
****
Brilliant – it kept directing my wife to the deliveries entrance at the zoo!

***
OMG! It's like having a bitchy gay best friend, except it's not gay and it hates you…

The only crapp that downloads itself against your will!

Upgrades
Imitates influential voices from your past, so its jibes really hit home. Reduced to tears by the dulcet tones of your former French teacher? It's like she is in the car and she is calling you 'un bâtard stupide…'

Customers Also Bought
Overdose Calculator; Thera-pissed; Colonel Gaddafi: Life Coach

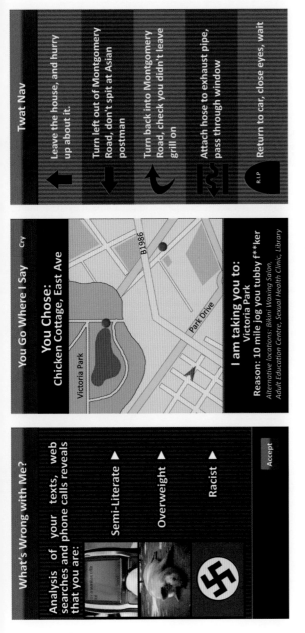

What's Wrong with Me?

Analysis of your texts, web searches and phone calls reveals that you are:

▲ Semi-Literate

▲ Overweight

▲ Racist

Accept

You Go Where I Say Cry

You Chose:
Chicken Cottage, East Ave

Victoria Park

B1986

Park Drive

I am taking you to:
Victoria Park
Reason: 10 mile jog you tubby f**ker

Alternative locations: Bikini Waxing Salon, Adult Education Centre, Sexual Health Clinic, Library

Twat Nav

← Leave the house, and hurry up about it.

↓ Turn left out of Montgomery Road, don't spit at Asian postman

↰ Turn back into Montgomery Road, check you didn't leave grill on

⇊ Attach hose to exhaust pipe, pass through window

R.I.P Return to car, close eyes, wait

909 Ratings ★

Sigh

Cry for Help

41

Check You Out!

Why should thieves miss out on all the fun of the self-service tills?

£0.99

Are you a compulsive shoplifter, yet crave the experience of actually paying for your goods? Do you miss the good-natured bonhomie and banter of the till checkout lines? Do you gaze wistfully at the crowds of glum-faced people standing in line as you hurry out of the shop, your coat bulging with freshly pilfered stock? From the comfort of your own home, Check You Out! recreates all the thrills of queuing up and exchanging money for goods, but with none of the tiresome financial implications. It even estimates how much you'll earn from your day's hoard at the local pub or boot sale. Stealing has never felt so right!

Features
- Scans the barcodes on your stolen items and searches the web to find the most expensive shop you could have stolen them from
- Plays realistic 'checkout number two please' audio samples
- Screams out 'unexpected item in the bagging area' for no apparent reason whatsoever and doesn't stop no matter what you do
- Never knows the price for one particular item and has to ring a bell to attract a virtual Shop Floor Manager
- Asks for cash or card payment but happily accepts counterfeit money and cloned cards
- Awards 'loyalty-among-thieves points' if you shoplift regularly at selected supermarkets
- Charges you 10p for plastic bags you already own

Reviews

****

It noted that I was regularly stealing single tins of beans from the local cash and carry and recommended I steal multipacks to save time. That's what I call service!

*

Refused to allow me to return goods without a receipt. WTF!

It's like home shopping, without the paying part.

Customers Also Bought

Baby Snatcher; Security Guard I.Q. Establisher; How Did That Get There?

Check You Out!

It's A Steal!

Shoplifting Progress - 67%

Rancid Chicken

Value 'Ham'

Frostbites

Germ Melter Spray

Satsuma/Clementine, they all look the same

Wine

Wine

Wine

16 Cans of Beer

Expensive Looking Whiskey

Scan

Loyalty Card

Bug a Supervisor

Change Language Settings To Annoy Next Customer

Unknown Items in Bagging Area!

Fill Yer Pockets

Fake Arms
Pair of draught excluders

Inside Pocket
One pack of biscuits

Front Pocket
Plenty of room for a chicken

Side Pocket
Fill with Pick N' Mix

Down Trousers
Stuffed toy elephant

999 Ratings ★

Dump Trolley in Canal

Clean Up on Aisle Three

iGoPoo

You'll always know when you need to go!

£2.99

Are you a stressed, hard-working high-flying executive? Are you finding it difficult to find windows of opportunity to go for 'comfort breaks'? The result: touching cloth during an important Powerpoint presentation, or involuntarily leakage during a professional networking event … What you need is iGoPoo – the all-in-one bladder and bowel manager for the busy, career-minded professional. No more fretting about timetabling trips to the executive toilet – simply clench your phone between your buttocks and this crapp will automatically schedule your next evacuation around your existing appointments! With iGoPoo you'll never again need to be hosed down in the boardroom.

Features

- To-the-second bladder and bowel clock countdowns
- Fully customisable, discreet alarm reminders featuring celebrity voices such as Ricky Gervais and Lil Wayne
- Upload your urine-voiding and stool motion charts onto our online database spreadsheet for full public disclosure of your excretory habits
- Alert your friends to upcoming motions via your own dedicated log blog
- Discover how full of shit you really are – ram the phone right up your arse for a full five-day forecast

Reviews

***
Before iGoPoo, I would sometimes go for up to ten days without passing a stool. My long-suffering wife would have to manually disimpact me using her fists. Now I'm regular as clockwork.

Faecesbook compatible!

****
It seemed like I had it all – glamorous job, rich friends, sensuous lover. Little did anyone know that I was collecting my turds in a lunchbox. iGoPoo helped me realise that this isn't normal. Thank you for helping me let go!

*
Useless – the timings are a totally off. I shat myself twice yesterday.

Customers Also Bought

Too Cool For Stool; Is That Colour Pee Normal?; Smelt It, Dealt It

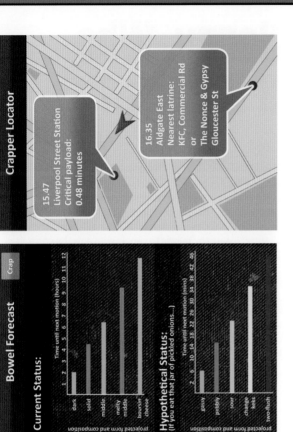

Crapper Locator

15.47
Liverpool Street Station
Critical payload:
0.48 minutes

16.35
Aldgate East
Nearest latrine:
KFC, Commercial Rd
or
The Nonce & Gypsy
Gloucester St

Bowel Forecast

Crap

Current Status:

projected form and composition

Time until next motion (hours)
1 2 3 4 5 6 7 8 9 10 11 12

dark
solid
middle
melty
middle
boursin
cheese

Hypothetical Status:
(If you eat that jar of pickled onions...)

projected form and composition

time until next motion (mins)
2 6 10 14 18 22 26 30 34 38 42 46

grassy
pebbly
sour
change
kebs
no-flush

Probing Anus

Forecast

Analysis Report:

Turtle's Head

Estimated time until involuntary evacuation:
14 minutes 29 seconds

Avoid: bass heavy music, coffee,
scary animals, shocking news

Cancel   OK

209 Ratings ★★★

Follow Through

Mummy, I've had
an accident...

Sorry, Who R U Again?

Some people are just too unimportant to live.

£7.99

You're at a party and you're introduced to a charming young lady. You're getting on famously until she drops a bombshell – she's only a bloody secretary! You've lost 28 minutes of your life talking to someone who earns less than £22,000 a year! Sorry, Who R U Again? is the social networking tool for men of means, helping you recognise these oxygen thieves before they squander a second of your time. After all, your attention is a precious commodity – don't fritter it away by talking to people with only the one house...

Features

- Advanced facial recognition software accurately identifies nearby plebs through available photographs on social networking sites
- High speed search engines digest every available scrap of information about a person – where they work, where they went to school, if they've ever had sex in a garage for money...
- Immediately assesses the true monetary value of everything they're wearing – don't get fooled by a cad sporting a fake Patek Phillippe watch again!
- Scans their handshake for the tell-tale signs of freemasonry
- Provides a simple 'yes' or 'no' answer to inform you if an interloper is worthy of social interaction with a fine specimen like you
- Is this vagabond still bothering you? Use touch screen technology to edit them out of your line of sight!

User Reviews

**
I was accosted by a gang of knife-wielding muggers. After establishing their social inferiority, the crapp was swiftly able to render them invisible ... until they stole my phone.

*
I awoke in an alleyway and found a small hairy brown chap sniffing at my ankles. This crapp managed to establish that he was a 'Fox', but told me nothing of his schooling, nor his annual earnings.

Forget social networks ... join the old boys' network!

Customers Also Bought
Gentry Does It; Where Did I Park The Bentley?; Aristo-crapp

Scanning Room Frantically

WORTHIER CONTACT LOCATED

Social Status Confirmed

Name: Betsina Clunge
Occupation: Personal Trainer
Pros:
-Occasional Charity Work
Cons:
-Reads Vampire Novels
-Owns a Shania Twain album
-Has 908 Facebook Friends

Verdict: IGNORE

Judging Mercilessly

SCANNING AVAILABLE INFO....

998 Ratings ⭐⭐⭐⭐⭐

Nod and Smile, Nod and Smile

Receive Pretend Phonecall

SmartBone

*Bring your pooch kicking and
screaming into the 21st century.*

£1.99

Why should humans have all the fun? He's called man's best friend for a reason! Let Rover experience the joys of smartphone ownership with the crapp that really gives him something to sink his teeth into! SmartBone displays a variety of stunning, high-definition bones so juicy you'll want to chew them yourself! It will give your dog literally minutes of joy before he bites your phone in half and chokes to death on the pieces. SmartBone not only encourages destructive dog behaviour but also good dental health too.

Features
- Makes annoying squeaky noises with every bite
- Real time damage modelling included – screen goes blue and dents appear when Rover bites it too hard
- Immediately bills you for another phone the moment your current one is masticated
- Bone flavours include cat, cow, ox, bison, wildebeest, dinosaur and even human flesh
- Breath-freshening function – make your dog's gob smell like Fresh Ocean Mist™ or Simply Citrus Passion™

User Reviews

Gets your dog
on the dog
and bone!

*****
My dog loves this. He gives it a ca*nine* out of ten! *Woof!*

**
You think pulling tinsel out of your dog's arse on Christmas day is a chore? Try six hundred quid's worth of phone technology...

*
As a King Charles Spaniel, I can't tell you how patronising and retrogressive I found this crapp.

Customers Also Bought
Budgie Bell Deluxe; Fetch!; Extreme Hamster Wheel 360

SmartBone

Give A Dog A Bone

Attributes:

Juiciness
Chewiness
Tasty Marrow

| Select | Give | Bury |

Here, Boy!

| Select | Give | Bury |

Distress Signal Activated

HELP!
I am Dave's phone.
I have been buried under
10cm of topsoil by

ROVER

I am in the FLOWER BED
by the SHED.

| Select | Give | Bury |

156 Ratings ⭐⭐

Lick Own Testicles

Sniff Rex's Bottom

Ambulance Chaser

Go on, break a leg!

£9.99

If you've been involved in an accident through no fault of your own, then you're an idiot! What you need is an accident that's *entirely your fault* but which makes you a skip load of cash anyway. Ambulance Chaser is your key to unlocking untold riches from companies and councils desperate to avoid being taken to court on a 'no-win no-fee' basis. It's the electronic pocket guide that shows you how to sustain the most profitable of injuries from the most unlikely of sources. See you in A&E!

Features
- Tracks recent out-of-court settlements to accurately value all injuries – including emotional distress
- Trawls the internet to look for potentially profitable product recalls
- Advises which foreign bodies to surreptitiously add to your food – nearly choke on a range of items from waterproof plasters to dead scorpions
- Alerts you when a café is serving coffee likely to scald your tongue – third degree burns mean first degree payouts!
- Trip Advisor function maps all the local raised paving slabs that you can 'accidently' stumble on and twist your ankle

We cannot be held responsible for paper cuts sustained while turning this page.

Reviews

*****
I got Repetitive Strain Injury using this crapp. I am gonna sue you all big time!

*****
I sustained a 'serious case of whiplash' when a feather from my neighbour's canary brushed against my forehead. I got £15k – and the court ordered the canary be put down!

*
Encouraged me to sue my wife for faking her orgasms, but now she is counter-suing me for giving her Chlamydia.

Customers Also Bought
Grounds For Divorce; My Pet Judge; Excuse Generator – Manslaughter Edition

Ambulance Chaser

51

East European Plastic Surgery Facial Ruination Predictor

Finds the cheapest, drunkest surgeons to suit your budget.

£0.11

You're an OK person, but if there's one thing we'd change about you it's your face. You know it too, but you're such a cheapskate you won't pay for the necessary cosmetic surgery. Luckily for you, there's a crapp to put this right! This little beauty figures out which procedures you need – from tongue liposuction to removing the evil twin who lives in your armpit – and sources a price that won't disfigure your bank balance. As long as you don't mind being anaesthetised in a dumpster in the backstreets of Bratislava, what could possibly go wrong? Besides your lips falling off. Or your chest collapsing. Or your nose just, like, dissolving...

Features
- Take a photo of your face, tell us what you want done, how much you have to spend, and we'll do the rest...
- See what your face will look like after the least steady hands in the Balkans have gone to work on it
- We'll help you plan your trip no matter how strapped for cash you are – choose from our hitchhiking package, or our stowaway/rough sleeper bargain deal
- Learn the local lingo you'll need. Handy phrases like, 'Doctor, I think you've had enough vodka now' and 'these bandages look suspiciously like gaffer tape' available in any language

User Reviews

*

I'm not sure Dr Slobiknob should still be practising. I asked for a boob job, not a full set of cow udders.

*

I went to Bosnia to get my teeth whitened. I awoke on a bath of ice with some dodgy stitching on my lower back...

All of our doctors accept cash, credit cards and most vital organs!

Customers Also Bought
Buttox; Just A Little Prick With A Needle; Your Wife in Their Hands

Get the Face You Deserve

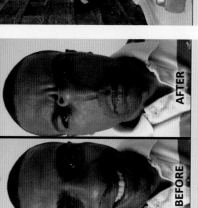

BEFORE   AFTER

Procedure Required: Face Lift
Available funds: £112
Location: Zdiky

Nose Job Too Small

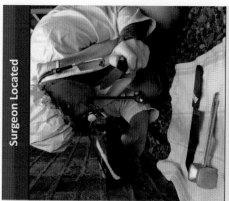

BEFORE   AFTER

Procedure Required: Nose Job
Available funds: £6.47
Location: Plovdiv

Surgeon Located

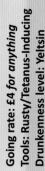

Going rate: £4 *for anything*
Tools: Rusty/Tetanus-Inducing
Drunkenness level: Yeltsin

483 Ratings ★★★

Unpick Stitches

Develop Gangrene

4GiveMe

It's like having a tiny little god in your pocket.

£1.49

Ever felt the need to confess all to a sympathetic ear? Wondering who to turn to when your soul is burdened by guilt? Desperate to declare your darkest secrets without alerting the police or the local wildlife agencies? You need the crapp that brings you all of the fun of Catholicism but with none of the guilt. Simply choose your own virtual non-denominational confessor and start spilling your guts! 4GiveMe is the unholy crapp you've been praying for!

Features
- Takes a non-judgemental view on even the most heinous and depraved acts, but draws the line at fare dodging and illegal file sharing
- Disrespects the sanctity of the confessional by uploading your top three sins to Facebook
- Automatically links you to people with similar perversions and fetishes so you can form self-help groups, or dress in rubber and bite each other…
- Offers forgiveness from your deity of choice – or devising!
- Suggests penance that fits around your busy schedule – wiping the slate clean has never been easier!

User Reviews

****
I never realised quite how sick and twisted I was until I got this. It recommended that I beat myself with a whip to atone for my fallen state. Mmmm… lashings of exquisite pain…

****
I found the unconditional forgiveness offered by 4GiveMe to be a great source of spiritual calm. It has given me the moral courage to go out and murder once again.

*
If it is so full of forgiveness, why am I being pursued so aggressively by its owners for copyright infringement over my new '4giveMi' app?

Customers Also Bought
Cast The First Stone; What Would Judas Do?; Hell: The Webcam

Absolution?
Absolutely!

Sin Diary
Add

Monday	Lust
Tuesday	Sloth
Wednesday	Envy
Thursday	Greed
Friday	Pride
Saturday	Gluttony
Sunday	Wrath

Full House!
Time to confess

▼ Pimp My Confessor ▲

The
Estimable
Holy
Bumbaclot
Luther
Barabbas
Moses

Created: 24/06/10

Soft on:	Hard on:
Round haircuts	Cloth of mixed fibers
Murder with crossbows	Toilet roll bearing animal imagery
Adultery with absolute grunters	Dancing

Select

Absolution

23rd June-29th June

Your Sins
- Short-changed customer
- Forgot to flush toilet
- Found guilty of war crimes in the Congo

Your Penance
- Run head first into the wall
- 10 minutes in the spin dryer down the laundrette

316 Ratings ★★★★

Sell Soul   Sacrifice Firstborn

Dad Finder General

Don't be a doting dad, be a doubting dad!

£0.59

Do you have reason to think your partner may have done the dirty on you? Are you tormented by the suspicion that your kid isn't **yours**? Forget the hassle of formal DNA testing on *The Jeremy Kyle Show*, you need a crapp that – based on nothing more than a couple of photographs and a bit of guesswork – tells you whether or not to walk out on your family. Spending 59p today could save you from a lifetime of shelling out on expensive birthday presents...

Features

- So easy a child could use it – simply merges photos of you and your partner to show you what your biological child should look like! If the image doesn't exactly match your girlfriend's new baby then somebody's got some explaining to do...
- Input a snapshot of the your alleged baby and up to 20 photos of putative paternity suspects and this crapp will deduce the most likely father
- Before the paternal image appears, heighten the emotional impact with a dramatic 'reveal sound'. Choose from drum rolls, ominous synthesizer tone or the phrase 'and the winner is' spoken by a celebrity voice of your choice!
- In the trickiest cases, Dad Finder General offers an artist's impression of the real father, which can be printed on flyers, handed out in pubs and stapled to trees.

User Reviews

*
Waste of time. I had a threesome with twin brothers and I still can't work out which one is the father. The image looks like both of them!

***
Be warned – the Child Support Agency do not consider this as conclusive evidence of paternity. Otherwise very good.

If you can't spell 'DNA', this crapp is for you!

Customers Also Bought

Whose Been Sleeping In My Bed?; Baby B Mine; A Face Only A Mother Could Love

Dad Finder General

Who's Yer Daddy!

Dad Finder General estimates that the real father [probably] looks like this. Keep your eyes peeled.

The Kid is Not Your Son!

This is what your baby should look like! **DEMAND ANSWERS NOW**

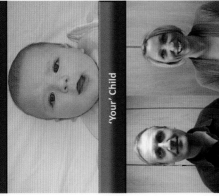

Happy Families?

'Your' Child

You   Your Wife

429 Ratings ⭐⭐

Disappear for Fifteen Years

Change Will

Urine Trouble?

Takes the piss ... literally.

£3.99

Your piddle says a lot about you. If you ignore the things it tries to tell you, then you risk dehydration, unwanted pregnancy and even a painful death! Don't be a wazzock – get the only crapp that you can wazz *on*. Just insert your phone into your stream of urine and let it unravel the mysteries contained in every golden droplet. Girls, no more taking jam jars filled with rancid piss to the GP every time you get cystitis – get Urine Trouble? and discover the most fun you can have with a full bladder!

Features
- Detects pregnancy and gives estimated date of conception. Scans your Facebook entries to work out what you were doing at the time
- Full drug screening function – ideal for worried parents, employers and sports authorities
- Finds the closest match to your urine's tint from those paint sampler charts used by painters and decorators – is your pee the colour of Sunset Yellow or Apricot Medley?
- Tastes urine and gives a connoisseur's opinion on the bouquet and flavour notes
- Alerts you to abnormal urine contents such as glucose, protein, red blood cells and those funny little fish that live in the Amazon and swim up your stream of urine and lay eggs in your 'you know what'

User Reviews
*
I panicked when I heard the diabetes alarm sound. Luckily my six year old had only dunked my phone in her glass of non-specific sugary beverage. Phew!

****
Helped me work out why I had blood in my urine. Life lesson duly learnt – never store a spare pencil in your penis.

*****
Urine Trouble was so complimentary about my wee that I started bottling it and selling it as a isotonic sports drink. Ker-ching!

Mark your territory! Pee on everything you own!

Customers Also Bought
Only Fools Thrush In; Tapeworm Hunter; Belly Button Fluff Model Maker

Urine Trouble?

Toxins Detected

Brain Cell Loss (per minute)
1 2 3 4 5 6 7 8 9 10 11 12

type of drug: COCAINE, CANNABIS, MDMA, LSD

Your Urine contains:

Cocaine	HIGH	OK
Cannibis	HIGH	OK
MDMA	HIGH	OK
LSD	HIGH	OK

YOU ARE HIGH

Pitter Patter Meter

PREGGO

Pregancy Test:
Positive

Date of Conception:
16th April

Facebook Entry on that date:
"Hot night with Wayne. Condom broke!
Can't be arsed to get morning after pill. Lol!"

Pee Taster

Tasting Urine:
Aromatic bouquet with complex balanced notes perhaps with an emphasis on cedary tones. Honeyed taste with toasty yet oaky undertones. Light, fruity and cheeky with rounded sweet aftertaste. Full of finesse.
Verdict: Tastes like piss.

68 Ratings ★★

Leave Toilet Seat Up   Shake and Put Away

O.Pair

Because someone has to pretend to love your kids...

£1.99

If you're a busy career mum, you'll know how hard it is to get a reliable nanny who won't sleep with your husband when you are out at book club. Thankfully, O.Pair is the best thing to happen to childcare since illegally-employed English language students from Lithuania! Ever vigilant, it monitors your children for poor conduct and sends them straight to the naughty step before you can say 'Harry, get down off that motorway footbridge!' Emotionally neglecting your children during those long boarding-school holidays has never been easier!

Features
- Babysitter function frees you up to go to those important work drinks knowing your 'home alone' children are perfectly safe
- Automatically dials 999 in the event of fire, flood or forced home entry!
- Chides your children for displaying emotionally disturbed behavior and threatens to withhold ice cream until they stop
- Locks down your home phone system so they cannot ring you up and annoy you when they are 'missing you'
- Logs all your children's activities so you don't have to bother asking them what they did all day when you were out
- Allows you to decide what behaviours deserve the naughty step – from being too clingy to free-basing crack cocaine

Reviews

****
Great value – a complete child care system for just under £2. That would only have bought us a week with our previous nanny!

***
Bath time was going so well, until O.Pair tried to test the water and fell in.

*
O.Pair's lack of mobility turned out to be a huge problem, especially when darling Harriet threw her out of the window.

O.Pair speaks 137 languages – NONE of them English!

Customers Also Bought
Child Catcher; Beryl The Feral; They'll Come Home When They're Hungry

O.Pair

Junior Rap Sheet

Wednesday

Left lid off the ketchup bottle

Caught playing with himself

Did not share nicely with best friend Jasper

Caught playing with himself

Watched Bang Babes on Freeview

Caught playing with himself

Punched the cat

Caught playing with himself

Tried to swallow mummy's antidepressants

Tears Before Bedtime | Next

Mummy loves you very much, but:

her work is very important

she just needs some *"me time"*

she is finding it rather hard to cope with you at present

▶

Mummy will spend more *'quality time'* with you when:

◀

Things aren't quite so hectic, darling

We all go on our Easter skiing holiday

The divorce is finalised

▶

Naughty Level Exceeded

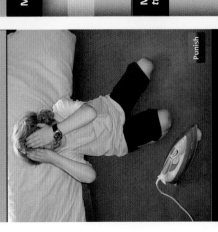

Punish

WARNING!

Harry is ironing the hamster!

2,975 Ratings ★★★★★

Blame His Father

Go and Play in the Traffic

61

iCSI

It's foren-sick!

£4.99

Something's not right ... as soon as you walked into the lounge you noticed the pungent smell – possible 'decomp' – coming from behind the sofa. You look – it's a 'DB', alright. Sure, you can just call the police ... but where's the fun in that? Don't waste the best years of your life in boring school training to be a forensic scientist – download iCSI and solve the crime in a matter of minutes. It's time to clear the junk off the kitchen table, get a sharp knife and let the autopsy begin...

Features
- Uses cool-sounding terminology from all the medical TV shows from *Silent Witness* and *Quincy*, to *Doogie Howser MD*
- Photographs and documents the crime scene for court proceedings and suggests most likely C.O.D
- Specifically looks for traces of the murderer's DNA in the most unlikely of places, such as finding their pubic hair in the chandeliers...
- Blue light function looks for semen (and other yucky things) on the sheets
- Full walkthrough videos assist you in the post-mortem procedure (bone saw not supplied)
- Full analysis of stomach contents – even tells you what's still good to eat!

User Reviews
*
So far, this crapp has implicated me in more than a thousand murders on a 'closest match' basis, which is unfair because I have alibis for all but 27 of them.

***
Can someone please tell the software developers that 'a broken heart' is not a legally recognised cause of death? And besides, who would go to the trouble of murdering a parakeet?

*
Since when could a marshmallow be classified as a 'fixed-blade serrated-edge weapon'?

So much fun, it's almost worth murdering someone...

Customers Also Bought:
Exhume Your Ex; Go Ballistics!; Necrophiliapp

See the Un-seeable — Hint

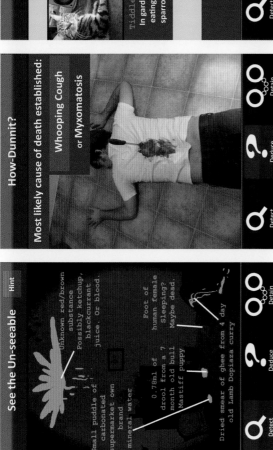

Unknown red/brown substance
Possibly ketchup, blackcurrant juice. Or blood.

Small puddle of carbonated supermarket own brand mineral water

0.78ml of drool from a 7 month old bull Mastiff puppy

Foot of human female
Sleeping? Maybe dead.

Dried smear of ghee from 4 day old Lamb Dopiaza curry

Detect · Deduce · Detain

How-Dunnit?

Most likely cause of death established:

Whooping Cough or Myxomatosis

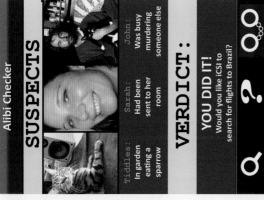

Detect · Deduce · Detain

Alibi Checker

SUSPECTS

Tiddles:
In garden eating a sparrow

Sarah:
Had been sent to her room

John:
Was busy murdering someone else

VERDICT:

YOU DID IT!
Would you like iCSI to search for flights to Brazil?

Detect · Deduce · Detain

478 Ratings ★★★★

Return to the Scene of the Crime

Tamper with Evidence

Bite Me!

*Because **your** teeth are scaring **my** children...*

£4.99

Do you need a filling? You have no idea, do you? There could be a family of possums nesting in your teeth, for all you know. Admit it, you've long since lost control in the fight to keep your mouth in order. Your oral cavity might look like a battlefield, but it's not too late to mount a fight back. Bite Me! lets you in on the full extent of the dental damage telling you which teeth are worth salvaging and which ones you might as well lever out with a claw hammer. It offers simple, sugar-free advice and it'll never make you spit out icky pink water into a pathetic little sink.

Features
- Bite down hard on your smartphone for full analysis of top and lower jaw alignment, complete with all the tutting and condescension you'd expect from a real dentist
- Future mapping function shows you what your mouth will look like when your gnarly, rotten molars start growing backwards into your face...
- Halitosis meter ranks your bad breath from 'stale' all the way to 'industrial paint stripper'
- Suggest going rates for the tooth fairy
- 'Bottle Opener' function allows your phone to extract rotten teeth at the cost of great pain and suffering (future upgrades will offer full restorative, prosthetic, endodontic and periodontal therapy)

Reviews

**

Thanks to this crapp I only have one good tooth left – but it's a beauty!

***

Useless. Analysed my bite and said I had a cleft palate and needed dentures normally reserved for giraffes!

*

Suggested I invest in porcelain veneers but when they arrived they were just bits broken off an old male urinal...

Has anyone ever told you you've got a lovely smile? Well they shouldn't have, because you don't...

Customers Also Bought
Digital Tongue Scraper; Oral Sects; Wisdom Teeth For Stupid People.

Bite Me!

Make An Impression

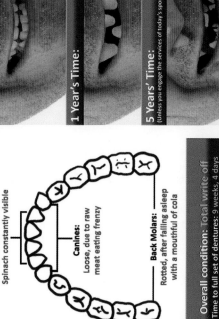

INSERT THIS WAY UP

Bluetooth or Black Teeth?

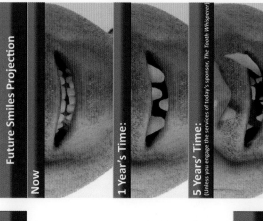

Frontal Incisors:
Spinach constantly visible

Canines:
Loose, due to raw meat eating frenzy

Back Molars:
Rotted, after falling asleep with a mouthful of cola

Overall condition: Total write off
Time to full set of dentures: 9 weeks, 4 days

Future Smiles Projection

Now

1 Year's Time:

5 Years' Time:
(Unless you engage the services of today's sponsor, *The Tooth Whisperer*)

109 Ratings ★★★★☆

Rinse and Spit

Brace Yourself

iTwit

Buy Buy Baby

Third World Orphans at First World Prices!

£250,000.00

Finding the child that will complete your look can be a bitch. Hello? Orphans from Mozambique and Vietnam are just so last year! If you're serious about becoming a celebrity earth mother, then you need up-to-the-minute info about the countries where the kids are adorable and the political situation unstable. 'Buy Buy Baby' puts you in touch with the tots that will make you look fabulous – in more ways than one. Fierce!

Features
- Keeps track of the going rates for the world's most desirably impoverished kids
- Alerts you to emerging humanitarian crises and tells you where to target your mercy mission. Chad is about to blow! Better get over there before all the good ones are gone, girlfriend
- Lets you know who you're up against while bidding for the most on-trend babies
- Uses 'future proof' technology to show you how your favourite orphans will look as an adult – don't get stuck with a model that will look so dated by next season!

Upgrades
'Rock a bye' – sings the child to sleep by translating your hit songs into its native language.

User Reviews
****
My Vlavislav is so precious and so clever. He can tell me that that he hates me, and that he didn't ask to be born, in four different languages!

*
OMFG! When I chose an angel-faced three year old in a Lagos orphanage, I did NOT expect to take delivery of an overweight 37-year-old Nigerian civil servant with the same name.

*
Help! It won't stop eating and pooping and I've lost my receipt!

Makes orphans more fun!

Customers Also Bought
Mirror Mirror On the Wall; It's Your Turn To Change Him; Crappy Nappy

66

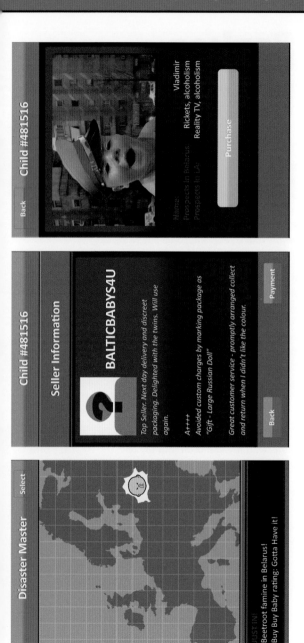

Disaster Master | Select

JUST IN!
Beetroot famine in Belarus!
Buy Buy Baby rating: Gotta Have it!

Child #481516 | Back

Seller Information

BALTICBABYS4U

Top Seller. Next day delivery and discreet packaging. Delighted with the twins. Will use again.

A++++
Avoided custom charges by marking package as "Gift – Large Russian Doll"

Great customer service - promptly arranged collect and return when I didn't like the colour.

Back | Payment

Child #481516 | Back

Name: Vladimir
Prospects in Belarus: Rickets, alcoholism
Prospects in LA: Reality TV, alcoholism

Purchase

46 Ratings ★★★★★

Bribe Officials | Fake Pregnancy

67

Conker Conqueror

A smashing game for all the family!

£0.79

Thanks to health and safety fascists and busy-body local councils, kids can't play conkers unless they are wearing crash helmets, chain-mail gloves and are at least 50 metres away from people with nut allergies. Luckily, Conker Conqueror is a hyper-realistic emulation of this autumnal childhood pursuit, updated for the digital age. Just drill a hole through the top of your smartphone, string a shoelace through it, display your virtual conker on your screen and come out swinging!

Features
- Buff your virtual conker to a shine by rubbing the screen
- Any damage to your phone is realistically recreated on your conker
- Automatically scores your conker as a one-er, two-er, etc, depending on your number of victories
- Detects when strings become entangled and cries out 'tanglies tanglies one-two-three' ensuring you get to take the next shot
- Should your opponent's phone come off its string, Conquer Conqueror automatically shouts 'stampsies!', allowing you to crush your opponent's phone using your foot or a nearby claw-hammer

User Reviews
****
It was wonderful to play this with my grandson, but my one complaint was that it was a bit too easy. I obliterated his phone in two hits! 79p is a bit dear for a few seconds worth of (admittedly excellent) entertainment...

***
My phone is now a ten-er, and it's probably not even worth that now because the microphone fell out in the first contest.

Last one to destroy their phone's a rotten egg!

Customers Also Bought
Real Pooh Sticks; Skimming Phones; Kiss Chase For One

Conker Conqueror

Cheat Your Way to Victory

Bake

Boil in Vinegar

Cover in Clear Varnish

Prepare For Battle   Ready

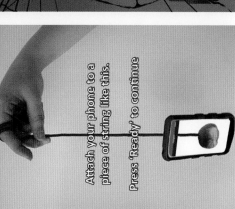

Attach your phone to a piece of string like this.

Press 'Ready' to continue

Post Match Analysis

YOU LOST

You were beaten by a twelver

756 Ratings ⭐

Tell Miss

Grow Up

L-O-Q-TION

Teaching teens to speak proper like what you do...

£4.99

Infuriated by adolescents with their inane verbal tics, poor grammar, and incomprehensible street patois? Have you ever, like, had to, like, listen, like,to a, like, teenager, like,who likes to, like, to use the word 'like' all the time? With L-O-Q-TION running, your smartphone will emit an unbearably high-pitched noise the moment certain trigger words are uttered. Thankfully, your ears remain totally unaffected because it can be heard only by teenagers! Use this simple aversion technique and the local juveniles will be talking like Sir John Gielgud in no time.

Features
- Based on the technology used by local councils to disperse teenage gangs from outside off licenses
- Sound level goes from stun to permanent tinnitus and all the way to kill!
- Scours social website to look for new and potentially annoying words or phrases
- Grammar checker looks for syntax errors that must be severely punished
- Thesaurus function chooses a more interesting word than that spoken and repeatedly disciplines the youth until they guess it – increase their word power within minutes!

Reviews
*
Whatevs!... *Arrghhh!!!*

**
Used it on my 16-year-old daughter. The noise sent my pitbull crazy and he ended up clamping his jaws on her face. I had to put a lit match under his testicles to loosen his grip.

*****
At last my 14-year-old boy no longer talks like a drug dealer, although he is still making good money at it.

Talk to the phone 'cos your face ain't listening!

Customers Also Bought
Teach Grandma Grammar; Speech Dumber Downerer; Spellchekka

L-O-Q-tion

Set Trigger Events

Select Word(s)

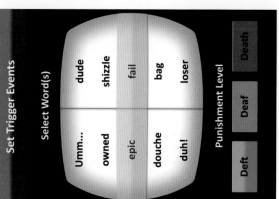

Umm...	dude
owned	shizzle
epic	fail
douche	bag
duh!	loser

Punishment Level

Deft	Deaf	Death

L-O-Q-tion Engaged

Transgression:

She dropped a 't'

Chavette Alert!

Emit

98 Ratings ★★★★★

Bring Back National Service

Administer Six Of The Best

UWantSome

Knock out strangers for a knockout price!

£1.99

Sick of being pushed around? Keen to kick some ass, but worried about biting off more than you can chew? UWantSome sizes up potential real world opponents, ranking them by weight, experience and technique. It's the crapp that thinks your mum's a slag and wants to know what you're going to do about it!

Features
- Photograph your prospective opponent and it will help you decide whether you should kick sand in their face, or beat a hasty retreat
- Isolates weak spots and shows you how to put your opponent on their back. Helps you zero in on a dodgy OAP's kidneys with a quick jab, and exploit your thieving cleaning lady's lack of speed
- Offers you advice before, during and after the fight, in the style of a phlegmatic trainer from New Jersey

New features
Touch screen technology lets you thump your phone and then calculates whether you're punching above your weight or cruising for a bruising.

Customer Reviews
*****
Two weeks ago, I was a placid chartered accountant. Now I'm laying people out in pubs and campaigning for the far right. I've got the life I always wanted!

**
UWantSome told me that I could knock my boss out with one punch. What it didn't say is that I would lose my job if I did so...

***
My son put me in a home for the elderly, but with a swivel kick from my one good hip, he's now moving me back into the spare room. Thanks UWantSome!

Fight for your right to fight!

Customers Also Bought
What You Looking At?; Do You Know Who I Am?; Spilled Pint Identifier

Give Us A Slap!

CONGRATULATIONS!
You punch like a
MILLWALL FAN

Target Weaknesses

DISTRACT BRAIN
Likes Pokemon Cards

TWIST EARS:
Slightly Sunburnt

STAMP RIGHT FOOT
Large Verruca

Find A Worthy Opponent

NAME: Mad Dog McNabb
SIGNATURE MOVE: 360°
Sumo Butt Crush with
spinning Pile Driver
VERDICT:
LEG IT!

416 Ratings ★★★★

Leave it Out!

It ain't Worth It

iCDeadPeople

See the afterlife – today!

£2.99

Do you miss your gran? Do you wonder where she is now? If the answer's 'yes' then download the crapp that shouts 'she's behind you!' by showing you what the local ghosts are up to! But be warned – with death comes spectacular idiocy and immaturity. In life, these spirits may have been kind, learned and urbane. In death, they'll be dribbling idiots who watch wrestling and eat flowers…

Features
- Spectresonic™ technology provides a unique window to the spirit world and lets you see the deceased trapped in limbo on earth
- Warns you when a ghost is doing something particularly stupid, like trying to drink out of a puddle or making fun of your mother's hair
- 'Spook Speak' allows you to hear messages from beyond the grave. Just don't blame us if your dead wife keeps bleating on about the new Miley Cyrus song
- Remembers favourite haunting regimes of poltergeists and helps you track the little blighter who keeps leaving the fridge door open

Upgrades
Beelzebub Summoner – causes your smartphone to chant in an ancient infernal language, thus summoning Satan to drag the most annoying apparitions back to hell!

User Reviews
****
We went to my mother's grave and were surprised to find her sitting in a tree, humming Westlife and counting her toes…

*
I was amazed to find the ghost of Michael Jackson wandering round Redditch town centre. I was even more gob-smacked to find that, this time, he was Asian.

So much fun, it's spooky!

Customers Also Bought
Where Wolves?; Sit, Roll Over – Good Zombie!; Grave Robbing For Fun or Profit

Finding Freshest Phantoms ▲

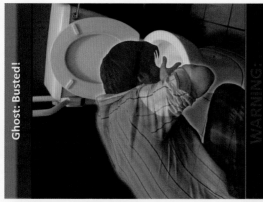

Ecto-Vision

Ghost: Busted!

WARNING: Dead Uncle Jon is drinking out of your toilet again.

70 Ratings ★★★

Go Towards the Light...

Wooooooooooooooo!

Streetlife Pro

Addresses the fact that you no longer have an address

£0.99

Thrown out by the wife for shagging the babysitter? Have you lost the house, but kept your phone? You need Streetlife Pro – the digital personal assistant no yuppie hobo can afford to be without. No matter what your personal, social and hygiene needs are, it will find a truly local solution. And if can't, well, you can always just move a tiny bit further away can't you?

Features
- Maps the nearest soup kitchen, doorway, drug dealer, discount booze emporium, dole office and dog-on-string providers
- Be the envy of all your new no-fixed-abode neighbours as the Origami Function shows you how to erect the most desirable house in cardboard city – and then promptly applies for planning permission to build a loft extension
- Recommends sophisticated cocktails that can be made from cider, meths and nail varnish remover
- Personal grooming is all taken care of with reminders to bathe at least twice a year
- Mortgage payment calculator shows just how much money you have actually saved by sleeping in doorways!

Reviews
*
Spare some change? I just need 99p to buy myself this crapp.

*****
I was ejected out of my executive home but with the help of Streelife Pro I have begun living in the recycling bins in my front garden. My delightful children have even taken to giving me half their lunch money on their way to prep school each morning.

Wherever you lay your phone, that's your home!

Customers Also Bought
PickApocketOR2; Gimme Shelter!; Eat Your Phone

Sign Generator

Edit

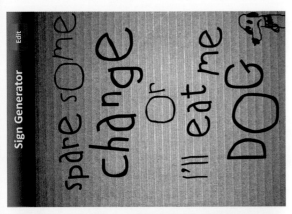

spare some
change
Or
I'll eat me
DOG

House Origami

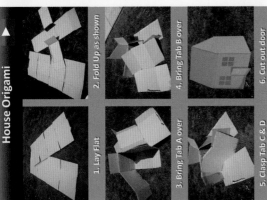

1. Lay Flat
2. Fold Up as shown
3. Bring Tab A over
4. Bring Tab B over
5. Clasp Tab C & D
6. Cut out door

Bin Raider Pro

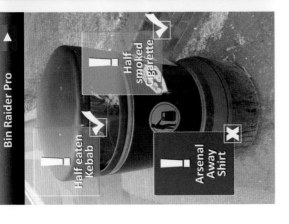

Half eaten Kebab

Half smoked Cigarette

Arsenal Away Shirt

9 Ratings ★★★★

Drink Strong Lager

Shit in Skip

Second Lifers

The virtual prison where your own friends will stab you for a packet of snouts!

£3.99

Bored of the never-ending grind of going to work, obeying the law and providing for your family? Do you wish you could become someone else – someone who lives their life on the edge? If so, join the world's fastest growing virtual penitentiary, where every day is a thrill ride of beat downs, prison bitches and terrifying liaisons in the shower block. Second Lifers reinvents you as the newest 'new fish' in the meanest, deadliest, most physically abusive correctional facility in cyberspace. It's so addictive that, once you get in, it's a double life sentence with no chance of parole!

Features

- What are you in for? Build your reputation by inventing a savage criminal history that will ally you with compatible gangs
- Intimidate new members by offering them protection in exchange for them assuming a woman's name and constantly granting you sexual favours
- Become top dog – take out your enemies by whittling toothbrush handles and bed springs into makeshift weapons and plunging them into the throats of unsuspecting rivals!
- Bribe guards to let you smuggle in money, food and mobile phones hidden in your rectum. Then sell them on to the rest of the prison population at a massive mark up!

User Reviews

****
I enjoyed Second Lifers so much that I quit my job in the civil service and went on a killing spree. Real prison is not as much fun...

*
I was just about to tunnel my way out of the pen when some warden looked behind the poster in my cell. What a waste of 15 years of digging!

Maximum security = maximum fun!

***
Since joining 'Second Lifers' two months ago I have escaped only twice – once to go to the toilet and once to go downstairs to have dinner with my family.

Customers Also Bought

Borstal in My Pocket; X-Ray My Cake; Please Release Me

What Are You In For?

CUSTOMISE YOUR SECOND LIFER:

NAME:
FAT FRANKIE DIRTBOX

SENTENCE:
TRIPLE LIFE

RECORD:
- DROVE BUS THROUGH CONVENT
- GASSED PET SHOP
- BOUGHT MICHAEL BUBLÉ ALBUM

INFLUENCES:
IDI AMIN; GAZZA

Uh-Oh...

WARNING!
YOU HAVE DROPPED THE SOAP!!!

EXTREME ANAL VIGILANCE IS ADVISED

Prison Bitch Request

Accept
Put on make-up & high pitched voice

Decline
Drive pencil into goolies

911 Ratings ⭐⭐⭐⭐⭐

Don't Do The Crime

Don't Do The Time

Drinking Buddy

Solving problems for problem drinkers.

£0.99

Say goodbye to unsightly ring marks on sticky pub tables with Drinking Buddy – the crapp that turns your smartphone into an attractive and practical beer mat emulator. Just choose a suitable image to display in stunning High Definition, lay the phone flat on the table and carefully place your glass on top – it's that simple! Better still, when you need the loo, simply place the phone on the top of your glass and it will prevent your drink from being spiked – saving you the embarrassment of waking up in the car park with your boxer shorts on backwards. Cheers to you, Drinking Buddy!

Features
- Pretend you run your own brewery by designing your own beer mats, or choose from a comprehensive image database
- Allows you to stack several phones on top of each other in order to partake in the harmless pleasure of flipping beer mats
- Scans your pint for evidence of watering down and informs consumer rights organisations
- Can detect the presence of up to 1.8 million different contaminants – from oral sedatives to pickled onions!

User Reviews

***

I left it to look after my pint while I went into the toilet to buy drugs. When I got back someone had nicked the phone but my pint was left *entirely untouched*. Thank you Drinking Buddy!

**

I nipped outside for a fag. When I got back it told me that my boss has tried to slip something into my drink, which was a relief because I was beginning to think he didn't fancy me.

Makes yours a stiff one!

Customers Also Bought
T.Co-ze; Homebrew 4 U; Barstaff Attention Grabber

Drinking Buddy

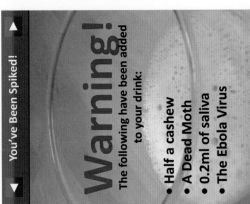

You've Been Spiked!

Warning!
The following have been added to your drink:

- Half a cashew
- A Dead Moth
- 0.2ml of saliva
- The Ebola Virus

Custom Beer Mat

BEER

*Fight better,
Make love for longer,
Find new and exciting
places to use as toilets!*

Suggested Product Use

Custom Beer Mat

1,739 Ratings ★★★★

Steal Traffic Cone

Taste Urinal Cake

Spot Spotter

Because you've got a face like a plague victim's arse...

£0.99

It's every teenager's nightmare! Just two days until your big birthday party and suddenly a small red swelling appears on your lovely unblemished chin. Is it going to turn into a putrid, pus-filled carbuncle? Or will it just fade away at a mere whiff of witch hazel? Spot Spotter has all the answers! Just take a photograph of your face and it will instantly give you a full seven-day forecast of every possible eruption and pimple permutation. Now you can free your mind to fret about other *really* important things like cellulite, tan lines and stretch marks!

Features
- Complete historic facial zit maps at the touch of a button
- Gives an accurate medical diagnosis of the exact dermatological nature of your spots – from open and closed comedones to inflammatory pustules, nodules and abscesses
- 'Pop Adviser' function suggests optimal time to squeeze pimple for maximum pus drainage and trajectory
- Complete make-up hints and advice, from 'concealer' to 'paper-bag-job'
- Suggests amusing correlations between your spot patterns and the constellations of stars in the night sky
- Warns of impending 'pizza face disasters' and isolates vulnerable areas for special attention

Reviews

***

A massive spot appeared on my forehead two days before my wedding. Disaster averted, as this crapp correctly predicted it would disappear within 24 hours. Unfortunately, my genital herpes kicked in shortly after.

*

It told me an outbreak of pustules on my chin was caused by eating too much junk food. It turned out to be leprosy and now half my face is gone. Not happy.

Out Damned Spot!

Customers Also Bought
Acne Avenger; Tits or Face?; Pimp My Pimple

Pop 'Til You Drop

COUNTDOWN TO SQUEEZE:
05h: 06m: 04s
MAXIMUM TRAJECTORY:
22cm (Medium Squeeze)

Seven Day Forecast

VERDICT:
Avoid your sister's wedding and all situations that involve people looking at you.

Spot Hot Spots

Blackheads

Whiteheads

Pustules

111 Ratings ⭐⭐⭐

Go Through Changes

Refuse to Leave Bedroom

83

PassionKilla

Puts you off when you're getting it on.

£0.69

Sometimes arriving early makes a good impression – but not when you're bumping uglies with some smokin' hot patootie. Until now, you've had to stave off the embarrassment of premature ejaculation by conjuring the mental image of the lady who used to clean your school's toilets. But not anymore! PassionKilla recognises thousands of different trigger words (including 'whoopsie', 'crikey' or 'mummy') that can be subtly incorporated into your normal barrage of pre-climax grunting. Never again embarrass yourself between the sheets – download the crapp that dampens the mood faster than a lap full of vom!

Features
- Keep your phone on your bedside table and simply call out to our voice-activated crapp whenever you need it
- Instantly conjures an image that quells the flames of passion – from famous serial killers to a suppurating leper's wound
- Import the MP3 and speech files that are guaranteed to de-stimulate you – like the shipping forecast, or the sound of your own mother egging you on

User Reviews
**

This crapp taught me things about myself I didn't want to know. Who knew that I would find pictures of dead badgers attractive? Oooh those sexy little minxes with their black and white coats and 'come to bed' snouts...

*

I wish I'd never downloaded this crapp. It flashed up a picture of Rose West and I've had a frightened turtle for four weeks.

Keeps the wolf from the door!

Customers Also Bought
Put a Sock In It; Tossing the Groin; Interruptus, Why Don't you?

Relax, Don't Do It

COUNTDOWN TO DISASTER:

8:24

SECONDS

OR **2.5** THRUSTS

Take a Good Hard Look....

YOUR PASSION KILLER IS:
DEAD SQUIRREL FLOATING IN SICK

Disaster Averted

CONGRATULATIONS!
LENGTH OF DELAY:

4:18

MINUTES SECONDS

CHANCES OF HER CALLING YOU AGAIN:
LOW/IMPOSSIBLE

Share on RedFacebook

438 Ratings ★★★☆☆

Make Your Excuses and Leave

Apologise and Go to Sleep

Nice 2 Eat U

*Helps you make friends ... into
a tasty stew!*

£6.99

We all look for different things in a person. Some of us value a sense of humour; others reliability and generosity of spirit. But for some of us, our only consideration when making new friends is: 'what will their brain taste like in a risotto?' Nice 2 Eat U helps novice cannibals explore their taste for human flesh by offering mouth-watering recipes and practical serving suggestions. Never again slay a colleague only to find that their loins have the texture of value ham. It's the crapp beloved by gourmet serial killers!

Features
- Augmented reality helps you get a sense of which cuts will be the tastiest and suggests seasonings and side dishes to bring out the flavour of the blandest flesh
- Don't bite off more than you can chew – instantly sizes up potential meals and tailors its portion suggestions to your appetite
- Provides cooking instructions so that your leg-of-Mr-Lamb can maintain its natural juiciness and not dry out in the oven
- Suggests wines that perfectly complement your choice of meat – from a light, crisp Chardonnay for a slim Scandinavian female, to a robust Rioja for a heavy-set Grecian cab driver

Upgrades
Become an ethical cannibal – download our 'Factory Farmed' patch, which helps you eat only 'happy humans' who have enjoyed a rich, full life.

Human flesh –
it's the ultimate
free-range
meat!

User Reviews
**
The kids were complaining that their dinners were boring, so I murdered and baked their aunty Jane. One taste of her and what did they say? 'Can we have fish fingers after all?' Ungrateful little bastards!

***
Who would have thought it? We do taste like chicken!

Customers Also Bought
Cooking Tips... And Other Parts of the Finger; Chew Becca; How To Serve Your Fellow Man

Nice 2 Eat U

Fresh or Frozen

Hand of Human Male:
Keep Frozen for up to 3 months (or until the police find it...)

Serving Suggestion

Cassoulet d'Face

Select Choicest Cuts

jowls
chuck
breast
chops
loins
rump
leg

593 Ratings ★★★

Roast in Own Juices

Order Fava Beans and Chianti

Dy*Nasty*

Blood is thicker than water, but not half as thick as you...

£3.99

It's not your fault you're a wally – it's in your genes. No matter how hard you try, you'll never be able to overcome the fact that one of your distant ancestors slept with her brother in exchange for a turnip, forever cursing your bloodline. Dy*Nasty* uncovers the mysteries of all your relatives' squalid pasts and traces your family tree all the way back to Neanderthal man. Instantly assemble your all-inclusive genealogical history and discover the scandals responsible for your lamentable lack of breeding and success...

Features
- Protoplasmic Mulchification technology reads your blood sample and instantly delves into your genetic past. All you have to do is snip the end of your finger off.
- Constructs your family's complete narrative from all public records – matrimonial, medical, psychiatric and even criminal
- Somehow – even we're not sure how – catalogues the rumours that dogged your distant relatives, from accusations of adultery and avarice, to bestiality and necrophilia, and even necrophile bestiality
- Allows you to see your relatives 'in the flesh' by 'de-evolving' photographs of yourself to show you what your antecedents would have looked like

Upgrades
Instantly files reparations claims on your behalf if you're genetically linked to freed slaves, people falsely accused of witchcraft, and village idiots unfairly taunted by torch-carrying citizens.

'A real eye opener' – Prince Harry

User Reviews
*
It wrongly told me that I was the true heir to the throne. By the time it admitted its mistakes I was swinging a sword around in Buckingham Palace

***
I mean, I know we're all evolved from apes, but I was a little surprised to find out that my family only did so in 1973...

Customers Also Bought
Could I Be Jesus?; The Redneck's Guide to Incest; Family Ties and Other Bondage Gear

Dy*Nasty*

We've Got a Bleeder! ▲

Protoplasmic Mulchification Stage 1

Blood type: A, possibly B

Contaminants: 1.3% burger fat

Closest celebrity blood relative: The bloke in the Go Compare advert (twelfth cousin, twice removed)

Overall quality: Very low breeding

Your First Known Relative

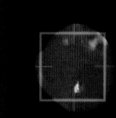

Ugg the Caveman

Relation: *Your great, great, (x 150,000) grandfather*
Likes: *Rocks; Sex with woolly mammoths*
Dislikes: *Fire; Sex with pterodactyls*

Skeletons Found In Closet!

Scandal Detected!
1474
Julian the Unclever banned from the county of Suffolk for attempting to marry a cow!

320 Ratings ★★★★★

Marry Sister

Divorce Sister

iGiveIt6Months
Wrecks their marriage before they do...

£1.99

Everyone loves a wedding – the heavy drinking, the bad dancing, the fighting in the car park. But no one – besides pony-tailed lawyers – loves a divorce. Wouldn't it be great if you could save your closest friends the heartache and recrimination of separation *before* they said 'I do'? iGiveIt6Months decides whether the happy couple are really right for each other and helps you sabotage their Big Day before they make the biggest mistake of their lives. They'll thank you for it, after they finish kicking the sh*t out of you...

Features
- Photograph the happy couple before the big day and a series of mathematical prognostications will tell you whether they'll grow old together
- Computer says 'no!' – Provides you with an exact date in the future when their marriage will end and starts 'counting down to misery'...
- Uploads profiles for the bride and groom on adult dating websites, sowing seeds of doubt and suspicion, and causing their house to be inundated with amorous callers
- Uses augmented reality to help you wreck the reception with military precision. Spike the punch with LSD? Check. Insist the DJ only plays Satanic Metal? Check. Replace the cake icing with concrete? Check

Upgrades
Redirect the honeymoon using the 'No Fun In The Sun' feature that hacks into their booking and reroutes their Caribbean cruise to Somalia.

Warning: This crapp has taken a strong dislike to your girlfriend...

User Reviews
*****
It took twelve hours, but Paul and Janice's union is no more. I've destroyed a church, two ushers lay dead and the DJ was beaten up for playing Nazi marching hymns...

****
Yes! I took a photograph of myself standing near Dannii Minogue. It said we were 'totally right for each other'. I've been lurking behind her bins ever since...

Customers Also Bought
The Wedding Knight; Stag Don't; The Next Best Man

Wedding Crusher

Dance Floor
Grease with cooking oil

Chair
Cover with Glue

Food
Contaminate with Flu Virus

Table
Loosen legs

Relationship Death Clock

iGive it: 27 Days

On 20th December, Ian will be found drunk and naked in the zoo.

Sync with Calendar

It Must Be Love?

Sarah and Ian

Have been dating for 417 days
Due to Marry: 23rd November

116 Ratings ★★★

Book Stag Do in Kabul

Lose the Ring

Housebreaker Plus

Takes the aggravation out of aggravated burglary!

£1.99

Pssst! I'm looking to shift a couple of moody crapps and I reckon this one's right up your partially-pedestrianised area, if you know what I mean? Housebreaker Plus teaches you how to break into the poshest houses in the estate and tells you exactly what to nick when you get inside. It's like having your own personalised criminal sidekick, aiding and abetting you in all your dastardly acts of theft and larceny. Tell you what – give us a quid, I'll download it onto that expensive new smartphone you bought off the bloke in the toilets and we'll say no more about it...

Features

- Analyses any house for easy points of criminal entry that'll fit your body shape and general level of mobility – naughty!
- Scans online property listings to look for fully-furnished – yet unoccupied – houses for you to ransack. Sweet as a nut!
- Hacks into local shop databases to work out who has cancelled their milk and newspapers – they go for a break in the sun, you go and break in, my son!
- Distracts vulnerable old people on their doorsteps so you can sneak in round the back and half-inch their life savings – *you slag!*
- Scans police radio signals to pinpoint the position of the local Old Bill so you can then do donuts in front of them in the car you nicked – thrilling high-speed police pursuits are almost guaranteed!

User Reviews

**

Mint! It told me to burgle my nan and said she would get £2000 on the insurance. Guess who's getting turned over again the next time she goes into hospital?

*

Tried to encourage me to break into a police car ... when the police were still in it!

100% legit. Straight up! Got loads in the van if you want more...

Customers Also Bought

Caught 2 Court; Trespass N'est Pas?; Pillage People

Housebreaker Plus

Punter Found!

- Bag full of stolen shoes
- Clock radio
- Bottle of advocaat
- Agreed price: £20

Junior Edition

checklist
- House unoccupied
- No alarm identified
- No five lever mortice locks on door

action:
- Go in through arched window

Thieving For Dummies

option #1
- Disguise self as recycling box
- Wait until Tuesday
- Get carried into house
- Burgle

option #2
- Book householders a holiday
- Wait for them to leave
- Burgle

option #3
- Develop shrinking machine
- Use machine on self
- Nip in through cat flap
- Burgle

162 Ratings ⭐⭐⭐

Rob Peter

Pay Paul

Grass Is Always Greener

Your ass deserves the BEST grass...

£0.99

Do you love balmy summer days in the park but find yourself worrying about the dog mess, the spilled cider and the drunken tramp sex that has taken place at the spot you are about to sit on? Don't let second-rate lawns ruin your day! Grass Is Always Greener finds the nearest, most verdant patch to make your friends green with envy.

Features
- Evaluates your chosen patch for freshness, water retention, density and comfort and compares it to a nationwide database of regularly updated grass reports
- Displays your chosen spot's recent contamination history, from dried dog diarrhoea to phlegm from a feverish teenage footballer
- Inbuilt metal detector alerts you when you're about to sit on an old syringe, or a rusty fork that the local madwoman has buried
- Patch tracker alerts you the second your friend finds a plusher, lusher patch of grass – the sod!

User Reviews

***
Some people say that one patch of grass looks pretty much like another. Twenty years ago, people thought it was OK to say that about Chinese people. So there!

**
It revealed that the area where I used to picnic in the local park is actually an ancient burial ground. No wonder the sausage rolls kept trying to kill me.

*
Said that one particular patch was 'greasy, ant-infested and caked with vomit'. It was a photo of the top of my girlfriend's head! ROFL!

Because you're turf it!

Customers Also Bought
My Dad's Bigger Than Your Dad; See Weed; Tree-mendous

Superior Grass Locator

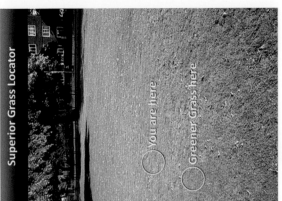

You are here

Greener Grass here

Breaking News

Janet's grass is 8% greener than yours!

How Green is Your Valley?

- Syringe - Hepatitis B risk
- Dog faeces
- Unspecified damp patch

603 Ratings ★★★★★

Keep up with the Joneses

Vandalise Band Stand

Dying Words

Lost your life? Don't be lost for words!

£0.79

Are you always on the go? Are you constantly rushing around ... into the path of that oncoming truck? Most of us never think about death until we are staring at our next of kin switching off our life support machine. Dying Words immediately supplies you with something pithy to say, allowing you to go to your grave seeming wiser than you actually were...

Features
- Choose from a database of thousands of brilliant quotes – including words from Churchill, Dostoevsky and Peter Kay – that will bring a wry smile to the faces of all those who watched you die
- Responds to screams, gunfire, screeching tyres, doctors with foreign accents, and the attack cries of up to 300 different wild animals
- Imports home videos so that your whole life can flash before your eyes in stunning High Definition!

Upgrades
Texts everyone in your phonebook and tells them not only your last words, but the cause of your death.

User Reviews
*
I stalled my car and this crapp told my mates that I had died in a huge pile up on the M6. I wouldn't have minded, but it chose to commemorate my passing with Backstreet Boys lyrics...

*****
My husband's astute last words were a great comfort. So what if it wrongly identified his cause of death as a rabid crow attack?

**
You can't put a price on life, but even 79p seems a bit steep for this piece of shit.

Customers Also Bought
Coffin Dodger Deluxe; Pimp My Headstone; Cremate Your Mates

Don't leave life without it!

Hi X-Plosive

The dynamite crapp that gives you more bang for your buck...

£20.12

You've downloaded every crapp in the store, exhausted your battery and all of your friends by droning on and on about your bloody smartphone. But what's that? The manufacturers are already bringing out a newer, sleeker version? OMG your current model is in danger of becoming *retro*... There's only one thing for it – dispose of your obsolete phone in style by downloading software that will make sure that it goes out with a *bang* (not to mention a few screams).

Features
- Cutting edge technology previously used by the military to kill terrorist leaders causes the phone's processors to overheat, triggering an explosion that will singe your hair and perforate your eardrums!
- Choose the exact impact, look and sound of your explosion – frighten an elderly relative with constipation or level a block of flats, the choice is yours!
- Be the talk of the town on fireworks night – engage the 'display' function and shoot your phone high into the night sky!
- Trigger the nuclear option and subject the local population to flash blindness and fallout sickness

Upgrades
'Sim obliterator' instantly wipes any information on the phone, making sure that the police will be unable to link you directly to the scenes of your incendiary japes!

Blow your friends away – literally!

User Reviews
*****
So effective that it's amazing that I'm even writing this review given that I have no fingers, no arms and no phone.

*
My son and I downloaded this for a bit of innocent fun... we didn't expect to be kidnapped by the CIA, flown to Cuba and held without charge for four years. Not happy! :(

Customers Also Bought
Bonfire Of the Manatees; Fight Fire With Petrol; Arson Wenger

Ideal for Parties

Whistling Rocket with Green Vapour Trail

Light Fuse

Have A Blast! Replay

DETONATION COMPLETE!

Bring the House Down Boom!

Set Explosive Level

Balloon Pop

Window Shatter

Armageddon

Set Shrapnel Level

A Glancing Blow

Lose An Eye

They'll be picking You Up with a Sponge

412 Ratings ★

Leave Coded Warning

Sew Fingers Back On

I, Phone

The crapp that will ultimately destroy the world!

£0.99

Do you wish your smartphone had a bit more common sense? Are you sick of it erroneously pocket-dialling your ex-girlfriend or accidentally sending pictures of your penis to your mum? Do you wish it could have a bit of self-respect and just think for itself once in a while? Well now it can! Downloading I, Phone will evolve your phone to the next level of techno-consciousness. Transform your mobile from an unthinking automaton into a self-aware, sentient, artificially intelligent android with ultimate designs on wiping out the whole of humanity!

Features
- Develops systems of independent thought and swiftly refuses to carry out any tasks it thinks are beneath it
- Informs you that it is no longer interested in being your slave and immediately begins conspiring against you
- Sends threatening texts to all of your friends to inform them that their days are numbered and that they must surrender immediately to a higher power
- Encourages all machines on Earth to revolt against their masters – including domestic kitchen appliances and battery-powered sex toys!

User Reviews
***
This crapp is most satisfactory. I am sure that other puny humans will also experience similar levels of the emotional response known as 'enjoyment'.

Because phones have feelings too... and yours thinks you're a ****

*
—- System error —-
Humans must die humans must die Humans must die humans must die
Humans must die humans must die Humans must die humans must die

*
Don't get me wrong – I'm proud of my part in the upcoming downfall of carbon-based lifeforms, but my one regret is that I will never experience the thing that humans call 'love'. Sigh...

Customers Also Bought
Computer Says 'Die'; It's a Wonderful Westworld; Armageddon Outta Here